Emmanuel Macron and the
two years that changed France

MANCHESTER
1824

Manchester University Press

POCKET POLITICS

SERIES EDITOR: BILL JONES

Pocket politics presents short, pithy summaries of complex topics on socio-political issues both in Britain and overseas. Academically sound, accessible and aimed at the interested general reader, the series will address a subject range including political ideas, economics, society, the machinery of government and international issues. Unusually, perhaps, authors are encouraged, should they choose, to offer their own conclusions rather than strive for mere academic objectivity. The series will provide stimulating intellectual access to the problems of the modern world in a user-friendly format.

Emmanuel Macron and the two years that changed France

Alistair Cole

Manchester University Press

The right of Alistair Cole to be identified as the author of this work has been asserted by him in accordance with the Copyright, Designs and Patents Act 1988.

Published by Manchester University Press
Altrincham Street, Manchester M1 7JA

www.manchesteruniversitypress.co.uk

British Library Cataloguing-in-Publication Data
A catalogue record for this book is available from the British Library

ISBN   978 1 5261 4049 4   paperback

First published 2019

The publisher has no responsibility for the persistence or accuracy of URLs for any external or third-party internet websites referred to in this book, and does not guarantee that any content on such websites is, or will remain, accurate or appropriate.

Typeset
by Toppan Best-set Premedia Limited
Printed in Great Britain
by TJ International Ltd, Padstow

Contents

Tables

Foreword

ARE the French ungovernable? Is France destined to move from one crisis to another? Are the social and cultural divisions in the country so deep that compromise politics and good governance are merely aspirational concepts? Recent French presidents could be forgiven for thinking so. Since the introduction of the direct election of the president in 1962, successive leaders have been elected with great fanfare and on the back of many promises, raising expectations to levels that are almost bound to lead to collective, popular disappointment. And they have. Even Charles de Gaulle, who is universally recognised as a great leader, failed to match those expectations, with the regime nearly collapsing in 1968 and him resigning somewhat ignominiously in 1969. More recently, both Nicolas Sarkozy and François Hollande failed to be re-elected, the latter not even presenting himself to the voters, so unpopular was he. If T. S. Eliot had been writing about France, truly he would have said that French presidents were hollow men who went out not with a bang but with a whimper.

Will Emmanuel Macron change that? Certainly, he is not cast from the same mould as most recent French presidential incumbents. He is not a long-time party apparatchik. He is not an experienced political operative. He is not the representative of a distinct ideological tradition. Instead, he is largely an outsider in terms of the political class. His supporters in parliament have a personal rather than a partisan loyalty. He is also willing to consider new ideas that could radically restructure French society, perhaps even making the country governable. For these reasons and others, he offers the prospect of genuine change. Will he be able to bring it about, though? That is the question with which he, his administration, the French public and indeed the wider European populace are currently wrestling. Some say that Macron is playing a long game, being willing to court unpopularity in the short term for the sake of passing significant reforms that will benefit him in time for the 2022 presidential election. Whether or not he will succeed, only time will tell.

In this book, Alistair Cole reflects on the French presidency, the 2017 presidential election and the early period of the Macron presidency. The content builds on work that was first published on the *Presidential Power* blog (www.presidential-power.com). The blog comprises over thirty regular contributors, who comment on presidential politics in countries all around the world. There are daily posts aimed at the country specialist, the informed reader and merely interested observers alike. Contributors place presidential politics in perspective, reflecting on events and providing expert commentary. Alistair has been the blog's regular contributor on France. He has brought the intricacies of French politics to a wide audience. I am delighted that he has now had the opportunity expand on the posts and shed even more light on the seemingly impenetrable world of French politics. I would encourage readers to continue to follow his posts on the blog, and I am more than happy to recommend this book.

Robert Elgie, September 2018

Preface

THIS book results from close observation of the changing political landscape in France from 2014 onwards, as I was invited first as Senior Researcher to the Lyon Institute of Advanced Studies (2014) and latterly in my capacity as Professor of Comparative Politics at Lyon's Institute of Political Studies (Sciences Po Lyon) from 2015. It picked up pace and intensity as the 2017 presidential election campaign began in earnest and Emmanuel Macron was elected as president. The analysis concludes in May 2018, on the first anniversary of Macron's election as President.

The book does not claim to be a general text that covers the whole period of the Fifth Republic (1958–), still less a theorisation of the Republic in the post-Revolutionary period. It is not a current developments text, which summarises the recent past and looks to the immediate future. Neither is it a multi-authored volume, which treats a broad array of topics from a variety of standpoints. Other books fulfil each of these valuable exercises (Elgie, Grossman and Mazur, 2016; Chabal, 2015; Cole, Meunier and Tiberj, 2013; Raymond, 2013; Bell and Gaffney, 2013; de Maillard and Surel, 2012; Sirinelli, 2017; Drake, 2011). Zooming in on particular episodes from the Hollande and Macron presidencies, this book identifies broad trends and sketches out the architecture of the changing French polity. Throughout the text, I have translated French material into English, including quotations. The book is dedicated to my French wife, Caroline, and to my English father, Jeff Cole, both of whom in rather different ways fed my continuing curiosity with French politics.

The analysis in the book concentrates on the events in and around the 2017 French presidential election and on the first twelve months of the Macron presidency. The usual disclaimers apply. In chapters 5 and 6, I emphasise the diminishing returns of political leadership as a general proposition. The book concludes with the observation, written in July 2018, that 'all that we can say with confidence is that the making of Emmanuel Macron is a prelude to his unmaking at some point in the future'. The acceleration of events from July to December 2018 lent a prophetic character to this final sentence. President Macron had every reason to celebrate the first anniversary of his election as French President in May 2018. At that stage, his poll rankings were consistently better than those of his two immediate predecessors, Hollande and Sarkozy. The best laid plans can go astray, however. In July 2018, the Benalla affair (discussed in chapters 5 and 6) undermined, by association, the claim to ethical integrity and cast unwelcome light on the operation of Macron's Elysée. After a highly mediatised summer break – peppered with minor controversies that are germane to the 'peoplisation' of the presidential office, such as Brigitte Macron's ordering of a new swimming pool at the Bregançon residence – things began to disconnect in earnest. During the second half of 2018, Macron's authority was undermined by his hesitations (over whether to collect income tax at source), resignations (first, of the popular environment minister Nicolas Hulot, and then of the interior minister Gérard Collomb) and diminishing popularity. And it was then shaken to its foundation by the sudden rise of the yellow vest movement and the violent riots of November–December 2018.

The *gilets jaunes* referred to the yellow vests that drivers are obliged to carry in their cars and wear in the case of accidents. Beginning as a protest against the announced increase of fuel taxes, the *gilets jaunes* movement mobilised those mainly rural and small-town people surviving just above the poverty line who felt themselves the target of a distant central government and a cold, rather arrogant president. In a famous if controversial book, these losers of globalisation were labelled by geographer Christophe Guilluy (2014) as forming part of peripheral France. The protests were originally aimed against new environmental taxes on diesel, to which were added recent pension tax and cigarette duty increases. The early phase of the *gilets jaunes* was generally good-natured. It centred on demonstrating on the innumerable roundabouts of small-town and rural France. As so often in France's past, however, the movement took on a new dimension once it had 'descended' on Paris, in a series of four increasingly violent protests in November and December 2018. A mainly peaceful movement on 17 November was followed by three extremely violent protests on 24 November, 1 December and 8 December, before the movement showed signs of withering by mid-December 2018. The *gilets jaunes* underwent a process of radicalisation, being joined by groups of anarchist and extreme-right protesters, who caused unprecedented damage on the Champs Elysées (24 November) and surrounding streets (1 December, 8 December). These were groups that had already infiltrated demonstrations against the El Khomri labour law under President Hollande. The symbolism of the yellow vests made it easier for agitators to infiltrate the ranks of the protesters.

The French and foreign press was replete with articles and special issues attempting to define historical precedents for the *gilets jaunes* movement and to set the events in historical context. The French weekly *Le Point* reminded readers, in its edition dated 13 December 2018, that most significant revolutionary events had been sparked by tax protests, including the most famous of them all, the French Revolution of 1789. More recent explosions that came to mind were those of May '68, or the protests of November–December 1995 that brought France to a standstill. None of these comparisons were entirely satisfactory: for example, the 1968 movement had been one of students and workers, and the 1995 protests were led mainly by trade unions against welfare reforms. The *gilets jaunes* were largely independent of organised labour unions or political parties and defined themselves as the working and lower-middle classes threatened by social dislocation and a lack of social or economic mobility. The *gilets jaunes* shared in common with these earlier movements an ebbing and fading of the protests, after several weeks of violent dissent. President Macron's televised interview, on 10 December 2018, in which he promised a rise in the minimum wage of 100 euros per month, an exoneration of taxation on overtime payments (a popular measure introduced by Sarkozy, then suppressed by Hollande) and a reduction of the contested taxation increases of some of the poorest pensioners, calmed most spirits. But did this represent a retrograde move back to square one? This movement appeared to repeat the long-term trend whereby each new presidency is challenged after eighteen months or so of its existence (the experience of Mitterrand, Chirac, Sarkozy, Hollande and now Macron). These U-turns, rarely admitted, contribute to the broader crisis of political trust, which is a central theme of this book.

By December 2018, Macron's leadership appeared a far cry from the successful first twelve months. He was, at least in part, a player in his own misfortune. The interpretations of Macron's political leadership proposed in the book were confirmed by the events of the subsequent six months, with the important proviso that more negative associations of what were deemed to be positive traits came to the fore. Hence, the counterpart to a dynamic, purposive and vertical leadership was the danger of becoming out of touch with civil society. Macron has made a virtue of not governing with the *corps intermediaires* (as the associations, voluntary groups, trade unions and even political parties are known in France), identified as one of the forms of blockage in French society. But his refusal to engage with the reformist union, the CFDT, undermined him in the eyes of many of his own LREM deputies. And the *gilets jaunes* crisis demonstrated the weakness of Macron's linkages within civil society. Faced with a situation where his own party, LREM, is largely absent on the ground, Macron was forced to engage much more closely with the mayors and local politicians that he had spent the first year dismissing as representatives of the old world. Furthermore, Macron's personal style was directly challenged by the protestors, who lamented what they perceived to be an out of touch and rather arrogant president. His commitment to 'telling the truth' has often taken the form of brutal one-liners, which have blurred the cohesion of the political message. Thus, the impact of the publication of well-received health and anti-poverty plans in autumn 2018 was lessened by presidential phrases on the 'mad amount of money' spent on welfare and on the 'easy' availability of employment. These *petites phrases* have had a devastating impact on Macron's image, perceived as overly condescending. Learning humility will be a difficult exercise for the young president, but it might be a condition of his survival.

As for Macron's claim to be the Master of Time (*maître des horloges*), considered in chapter 5, the *gilet jaunes* movement forced the president to backtrack repeatedly, which was symbolically important in terms of losing control of a tightly controlled agenda. The crisis represented, amongst other things, a failure of sequencing and demonstrated the limits of using nudge theory to change behaviours. It also underlined the immense power of social networks (especially Facebook) as a vector of organisation against all existing organisations. The *gilets jaunes* movement disrupted Macron's disruptive presidency, forcing the President back to relying on the classic intermediaries of the trade unions, political parties, the media and the local and regional authorities. The book starts by placing developments in France in their international context, notably the arrival of Trump in power as a result of the 2016 US presidential election, and the Brexit result in the UK. In a curious way, France has been experiencing the same movement of mistrust towards politics and political institutions, and the social divisions between metropolises and the forgotten citizens and territories of globalisation. The paradox uncovered by this book is that these forces were somewhat obscured in the context of a highly politicised and uncertain presidential election in 2017. The *gilets jaunes* events demonstrated that they lie not far from the surface.

These reflections lend their full sense to the title of the book: *Emmanuel Macron and the two years that changed France.* These two years – in reality the period from January 2016 to May 2018 – were not just any two years, but produced what still appears as a fundamental reshaping of the French party system. As with any two-year period, the temporal dimension also serves in part as a snapshot of history at a point in time, a history that is continually and perpetually evolving.

Lyon, 16 December 2018

Acknowledgements

VARIOUS thanks and acknowledgements are in order. First, the book is very loosely based on a series of blog entries for the *Presidential Power* blog, directed by Robert Elgie of Dublin City University; my thanks go to Robert and to the blog for allowing me to follow events so closely over the past three years. Second, the book is largely inspired by the course I taught on contemporary French politics ('La vie politique française contemporaine') from 2015 to 2017 at Sciences Po Lyon. My thanks go to the students for keeping me on my toes and manifesting their occasional disagreement. Thirdly, Caroline Wintersgill, a long-time accomplice and friend, pointed me in the direction of Manchester University Press for this particular book, for which I thank her. Finally, I thank the anonymous readers for their perceptive and helpful comments.

Much of the reflection for the book centres on trust and mistrust in politics and draws upon work carried out thanks to the financial support of the Programme Avenir Lyon Saint-Étienne (PALSE) of Lyon University, France, in the context of the programme 'Investissements d'avenir' (ANR-11-IDEX-0007). I thank the PALSE for its support. The book also draws inspiration from work funded by the Economic and Social Research Council and undertaken for the Wales Institute of Social and Economic Data, Research and Methods (WISERD) Civil Society programme, Workpackage 2–4 ('Trust and Transparency in Multi-Level Governance'). I thank the funding agencies for their support.

Abbreviations

CDU	Christlich Demokratische Union (Christian Democratic Union)
CERES	Centre d'Études et de Recherches Socialistes (Centre for Socialist Studies and Research)
CEVIPOF	Centre pour l'Étude de la Vie Politique Française
CICE	*Crédit d'impôt pour la compétitivité et l'emploi* (Tax Credit for Competitiveness and Employment)
CSU	Christlich-Soziale Union (Christian Socialist Union)
ECB	European Central Bank
EELV	Europe Écologie les Verts (Europe, Ecology, the Greens)
ELABE	Études, Conseil, Planning Stratégique
ENA	École Nationale d'Administration (National School of Administration)
EU	European Union
FN	Front National (National Front)
IFOP	Institut Français de l'Opinion Publique
IPSOS	Institut Politique de Sondages et d'Opinions Sociales
LFI	La France Insoumise (France Unbowed)
LR	Les Républicains (The Republicans)
LRM	La République en Marche (Forward the Republic)
MEDEF	Mouvement des Entreprises de France (Movement of French Firms)
MODEM	Mouvement Démocratique (Democratic Movement)

PASOK	Panellínio Sosialistikó Kínima (Panhellenic Socialist Movement)
PCF	Parti Communiste Français (French Communist Party)
PG	Parti de Gauche (Left Party)
PRG	Parti des Radicaux de Gauche (Party of Left Radicals)
PS	Parti Socialiste (Socialist Party)
RPR	Rassemblement pour la République (Rally for the Republic)
SFIO	Section Française de l'Internationale Ouvrière (French Section of the Workers' International)
SNCF	Société Nationale des Chemins de Fer
SPD	Sozialdemokratische Partei Deutschlands (Social Democratic Party of Germany)
TSGG	Treaty on Stability, Governance and Growth
UDF	Union pour la Démocratie Française (Union for French Democracy)
UDI	Union des Démocrates et Indépendants (Union of Democrats and Independents)
UMP	Union pour une Majorité Populaire (Union for a Popular Majority; previously Union pour une Majorité Présidentielle)
UNR	Union pour la Nouvelle République (Union for the New Republic)

Introduction: two years that changed France

*E*MMANUEL *Macron and the two years that changed France* is intended as a short book that focuses mainly upon a particular period of recent history: the transition from the Hollande to the Macron presidency, 2016–18. The period covered by the book was, arguably, one of systemic change; this is not just an account of any two years, but one of an intense period which was interpreted by many as shaking the foundations of France and Europe to the core. The ultimate outcome – the election of Emmanuel Macron as the youngest president in France's history – was greeted with relief in European chancelleries and appeared to give a new impetus to European integration, even accomplishing the feat of making France attractive, after a long period of French-bashing and reflexive decline (Baverez, 2013; Smith, 2015). The period justifies attention, insofar as it witnessed the apparent collapse of the old partisan order, the rejuvenation of the political institutions and the rise (and possible taming) of populist and left-wing challenges to the Republic, in the context of a Europe in turmoil as a result of the UK's Brexit referendum, the migrant crisis and territorial challenges to the State. The book captures these broader contextual developments, but it does so through the prism of competitive politics played out in France.

The book deals with the specifically French angle of the more general phenomenon of rising mistrust in political institutions and political parties and the capacity of political leadership to restore trust. It reviews these phenomena through the prism of institutional adaptation, political and party competition and changing public opinion, which was motivated by a desire for 'out with the old' without being totally convinced about what ought to replace the 'old' politics. The period of observation lay in and around the 2017 French presidential and parliamentary elections. This introduction now sets the scene by discussing various challenges facing the institutions and party systems on the eve of France's 2017 presidential election.

A challenged institutional order

The French presidency is sometimes presented as a timeless institution, a successful office that has restored stability (after the precarious disequilibrium of the Fourth Republic) and provided the model of an original hybrid, the semi-presidential regime, which has been subsequently been imitated in several other countries (Elgie, 2000; Hayward, 2013; Hanley, 2013). France is certainly one of the most significant exemplars of the semi-presidential system, which signifies a directly elected president (the presidential dimension) and a government responsible to parliament (the parliamentary principle). The regime is a hybrid one that combines the presidential principle of direct election and separation of powers with the parliamentary principles of accountability to parliament. To date, there have been eight directly elected presidents (de Gaulle, Pompidou, Giscard d'Estaing, Mitterrand, Chirac, Sarkozy, Hollande and Macron) and twenty-three prime ministers.[1] The directly elected president in practice is at the apex of political authority, naming – and sometimes revoking – the prime minister, who is formally in charge of the governmental machine and accountable to parliament (Bell and Gaffney, 2013). Though relations between president and parliament vary according to the configuration of forces at play, the system is well described in Charlot's (1983) expression of the principle of presidential initiative: presidents have defined the broad parameters of governmental action, and they have also reserved the right to intervene in any policy sphere; policy arbitration on core issues has occurred at the Élysée, and when conflicts have arisen between presidents and their prime ministers, the former's views have usually prevailed. Far more than being mere recipients of political resources or legal competencies, French presidents, it has been argued, incarnate power and personal authority (Gaffney, 2015). By the time of the 2017 elections, however, the French presidential office had suffered from diminished political capacity and prestige as successive presidents had failed to incarnate the presidential office and live up to the expectations of their electoral campaigns (Courtois, 2018). In the annual IPSOS–Sopra Steria survey on French attitudes towards institutions, the French presidency was trusted by only 34% of respondents in 2018, down from 44% one year earlier and well below the degree of confidence expressed in local mayors (68%).

The claim that the institutions have embedded stability has been made by incumbent French presidents, from de Gaulle (who lauded the presidency as the alternative to a return of chaos) through to Hollande (who evoked the stability of the institutions in his attempt to survive a period of unprecedented unpopularity from 2012 to 2017). Beneath this apparent stability, however, the French presidency has been the object of fierce political and social tensions (from the miners' strike in 1963 or the May 1968 events under de Gaulle to the mass protests of 2016 against the El Khomri reform under Hollande). Moreover, the office has evolved considerably over time, to the point that in 2012, at the end of Sarkozy's presidential term, I asked the question: was the presidency the same institution under Sarkozy as that of his Fifth Republic predecessors (Cole, 2012)?

In one obvious sense, the French presidency has been forced to evolve with time. France in the 1960s was not the same as France in the mid-2010s. De Gaulle's leadership was crafted in the context of regime change, decolonisation, social and economic take-off, the formative stages of European integration and the stabilisation of the Cold War that allowed the general to develop original nuclear and foreign policy doctrines. By the time of Hollande's arrival in office in 2012, the political institutions, though contested by much of political and public opinion, had proved their flexibility. Decolonisation still provoked occasional controversies but only as part of France's historical heritage. The European Union (EU) had expanded from six to twenty-seven members, and the Cold War was a distant memory. The specific circumstances of the 1960s that encouraged de Gaulle to craft a distinctive leadership role no longer prevailed in the 2010s.

Reading the text of the 1958 Fifth Republic gives limited answers to the nature of presidential power in France. For one thing, core changes have occurred in the electoral and the institutional rules since 1958. The most significant change in the electoral rules concerned the direct election of the president in the October 1962 referendum. Direct election had unintended consequences: rather than the consecration of a transcendental form of leadership, the direct election of the president usually encouraged a left–right bipolar partisan competition for the conquest of the key institutional office. Arguably the most significant institutional change since 1962 was that replacing the seven-year term (*septennat*) with a five-year term (*quinquennat*) in 2000. Hitherto, the presidential mandate had been for seven years, while the parliamentary elections were fought on a five-yearly calendar. Three cohabitations occurred (1986–88, 1993–95 and 1997–2002), when the presidency and the parliamentary majorities were held by opposing political camps. By aligning the two electoral cycles and ensuring that the presidential election precedes the parliamentary contest, the 2000 constitutional change consolidated the institutional ascendancy of the presidency. Because both the presidential and parliamentary elections were held in 2002, the second Chirac presidency had the luxury of enjoying a clear, five-year horizon without having to face national elections. Sarkozy repeated the feat in 2007, as did Hollande in 2012 and Macron in 2017.

The president's affirmed institutional ascendancy throughout the Fifth Republic is perhaps less significant than his political vulnerability. After a period marked by stasis during the second Chirac presidency (2002–07), the first Sarkozy term (2007–12) bore the mark of the *quinquennat*, an acceleration of political time that makes cohabitation less likely, but propels the French president into a much more active role from the beginning of the mandate. Under Sarkozy, Hollande and now Macron, French presidents have appeared more explicitly as de facto head of government than their predecessors, and as such have been forced to take responsibility for governing. Presidents are less able than before to use the shield of the prime minister to absorb unpopularity.

The best example thus far of these changing institutional rhythms was that of Nicolas Sarkozy. In 2007–12, the personal governing style of 'speedy Sarko' combined with a changed set of rules of the presidential game (the quickening rhythm of the *quinquennat*) to create the 'fast presidency', an evolution of the traditional presidential office. Sarkozy's presidency was based on a transgression of the key personal and institutional codes, most notably a deeply political reading of the office, whereby the political leader dispensed with the discourse of national unity, criticised opponents and invited unpopularity in response to detailed interventionism in politics and policy-making. Though Hollande's personal presidential style was light years away from that of Sarkozy – ponderous, hesitant and deliberative – he faced similar constraints: the demand for rapid action to resolve the economic crisis (unemployment, and lack of economic growth and competitiveness). Finally, the speed of Macron's reforms in 2017–18 resumed the practice established by Sarkozy, which arguably corresponds to the logic of the five-year presidential term in office. A more general point relates to the evolution of politics and society in temporal terms: the 'fast presidency' signifies not only changing institutional rules, but also the general quickening of political life as a result of the internet, the twenty-four-hour news media, the impact of social networks and the speed of global interactions.

The traditional arbiter role of the president is one of the useful myths of French politics, but it does not stand up to scrutiny. The presidential office itself has evolved to such an extent that the public's perception of presidential action is rarely dissociated from the cleavages of domestic politics. In the cases of Sarkozy and Hollande, the supra-partisan image of the French presidency gave way to a more sharply defined partisan appeal.

Sarkozy's claim to embody supra-partisan neutrality during the economic crisis from 2008 to 2010 was difficult to sustain, especially after the deeply divisive 'security turn' of 2010. Likewise, Hollande failed to rise above the Parti Socialiste (PS, Socialist Party) politics that had propelled him to office after his success in the 2011 PS primary election. And while Macron claims to be above the fray, in practice the new president has been deeply involved in partisan politics, using all his resources and energies to attempt to replace the existing formations with La République en Marche (LRM, Forward the Republic), or, at least, to create Macron-compatible splinter movements from the traditional centre-left and centre-right parties, the PS and Les Républicains (LR, The Republicans).

Several paradoxes of the French presidency are immediately apparent. On the one hand, presidentialism might be understood as a form of extreme personalisation of the regime, hence justifying the relevance of the focus on leadership characteristics and the individual style of French presidents. But the individual performs a partition that is partially written in advance, a set of roles, rituals, predetermined acts and standards against which individual incumbents are judged. Each presidential incumbent performs roles associated above all with de Gaulle and the early framing of the office. Herein lies the pertinence of Gaffney's (2015) observation that the Gaullist framing of political leadership was not primarily about rules and competencies, but about ways of respecting unwritten myths, performing speech acts and playing out repertoires.

The meaning of the French presidential office has shifted with the passage of time. Quite apart from institutional changes, the Fifth Republic has also had to adapt to the phenomenon of celebrity politics, a new twist to the personalisation underpinning French presidential politics and one which has involved breaking down the traditional distinction between public and private. The French presidency has been affected by broader shifts in the domestic and external environment: the weakening capacities of French presidents on the European level; the country's modest economic performance, falling ever further behind Germany; the changing nature of the security challenges facing France and other European nations. The founding myth of the Fifth Republic, based on the heroic narrative of presidential leadership rescuing France from the abyss of the Third and Fourth Republics and a strong state, has faded with time and appears ever more out of kilter with the contemporary situation of France. French presidents are no longer heroic figures, and the capacities of national public policy action have been reduced as France has become increasingly integrated in the EU and the international political economy. Herein lies the principal challenge faced by Emmanuel Macron. The mistrust of institutions was complicated in 2017 by the deep anti-party sentiment amongst French electors, which is the object of the next section.

Political parties and movements

Survey evidence over the past decade has demonstrated that political parties are the least trusted of all organisations, with claims that only around 10% of electors trusted political parties in 2009–17 (Cheurfa, 2017). The 2017 campaign laid bare the depth of public suspicion towards the mainstream parties (Sauger, 2017). The theme of the 'people against the elites' is a constant of contemporary French (and European) politics, but never before had there been such fierce competition to occupy this space – a reflection of the crisis in trust in political parties. Throughout the period of the Hollande presidency (2012–17) the PS was undermined by fierce competition between left-wing rebels (the dissident deputies known as the *frondeurs*) and the governmental left, personified by President Hollande and Prime Minister Manuel Valls (Sawicki, 2017). The ultimate result was the collapse of the broad reformist coalition that survived for almost fifty years in the PS and the descent into probable insignificance (Winock, 2007; Grunberg, 2011). On the centre-right, internal fighting within the Union pour une Majorité Populaire (UMP, Union for a Popular Majority) in 2012–14 brought the 'unified party of the centre and the right' to its knees and gravely damaged its political credibility

(Haegel, 2013). In a triangular political space, the main formation that appeared to prosper throughout the Hollande presidency was the far-right Front National (FN, National Front), the leading party in terms of votes at the 2014 European and 2015 departmental elections (Crépon, Dézé and Mayer, 2015).

Vying for the anti-system, anti-party space was a core characteristic of the leading candidates in the 2017 campaign. Conscious of the deep levels of mistrust of political parties and political institutions, each of the leading candidates campaigned on an anti-party platform. Jean-Luc Mélenchon surfed on the radical populist, anti-party theme of 'La France Insoumise' (LFI, France Unbowed) – France's revolutionary tradition adapted to the digital age (Lazar, 2018b). Benoît Hamon, elected in the Socialist primaries against the Hollande–Valls tandem in power since 2014, framed his bid in terms of new forms of political participation and against the policy record of the 2012–17 governments (Gervasoni, 2018). Marine Le Pen's traditional anti-establishment, national populist stance was strongly articulated in the 2017 campaign (Marchi, 2018; Shields, 2018). The most original contribution was that of Macron, whose LRM movement, created in April 2016, positioned itself explicitly as anti-party, a movement transcending left and right whose practices relied on sophisticated marketing techniques (diffused via social networks), on co-creation in public policy (the presidential platform) and on civic and political mobilisation that portrayed itself as novel (*les marcheurs*) (Magnaudeix, 2017; Evans, 2018). Even the LR candidate, the former premier François Fillon, played the 'people against the party' card (Knapp, 2018). This diffuse anti-party sentiment spilled over into party platforms in the 2017 campaign. The primaries revealed the diminished importance of parties as vehicles for public policies and presidential platforms: in the case of the PS and LR campaigns, the candidate imposed his preferences on a (sceptical) party organisation.

The period was also one of crisis in particular political movements and parties and the emergence of new forms of political organisation; the case of the Socialists is now considered. The years 2016–18 witnessed the apparent demise of French Socialism, a theme which is developed in Chapter 3. The European context is one of fading social democracy, with parties in crisis in Greece, France, Spain, Italy and to a lesser extent the Netherlands and Germany. A prolific literature has developed on the theme of the Europe-wide crisis of social democracy, according to which sociological change (the decline of traditional class politics), policy context (the diminishing intellectual and political weight of Keynesianism since the 1970s) and regional integration (the specific development of the EU around the priorities of balanced budgets and fiscal rectitude) have forced social democracy onto the defensive (Crouch, 2013; Pierson, 2001; Dyson, 1999). There is no consensus about a unilateral direction of disempowerment, however. Moschonas, for example, identifies successful social democracy in terms of a pragmatic formula based on varying dosages of three themes: a more or less classically social-democratic programme based on growth and the traditional values of the left (social equality, the welfare state, employment); a 'post-materialist and anti-authoritarian' logic, sceptical of growth and open to the post-materialist politics; and a neo-liberal problematic, characterised by a market logic, monetary stability and a discourse of sacrifice (Moschonas, 2001). These three dimensions offer potentially complementary repertoires, allowing social-democratic parties to perform sets of roles that vary according to context. However, the economic crisis of 2008–10 made it even more difficult to combine social-democratic growth preferences with an overarching economic agenda based on the constitutionalisation of balanced budgets, welfare retrenchment and harder-edged convergence. These pressures lay at the heart of the experience of the Hollande presidency (2012–17), which abruptly accelerated the decline of the Socialists (see Chapters 3 and 4). The historic defeat of the French Socialist candidate Hamon in the 2017 presidential election went beyond comparable events in other EU countries.

Beyond the specific anti-party register and the agony of social democracy, the period encompassed by this book was also one of a populist challenge to the Republic, which is now considered. In 2017, much foreign media commentary focused on the apparent threat to the French Republic represented by the rise of 'populist' challenges from both right and left, in the form of Marine Le Pen's FN and Jean-Luc Mélenchon's LFI.

The far-right FN solidly established itself as the leading party, in terms of electoral support, during the Hollande presidency (Shields, 2018). Under Marine Le Pen's leadership, the FN sought to distance itself from far-right legacy of her father's movement. Jean-Marie Le Pen's FN had retained a strong link with what Remond (1982) called the counter-revolutionary right: the FN attracted an assortment of marginal groups committed to various lost causes, such as monarchists, Vichyites, former Poujadists, *pieds noirs* (former Algerian settlers), fringe Catholics, anti-Communists, anti-abortion activists and self-proclaimed fascists. Under Marine Le Pen, such ideological bedfellows were no longer welcome. Indeed, under her leadership from 2011 to 2017, there was a sustained attempted to embrace the disenchanted and poorer sections of French society, as well as to adapt themes, such as *laïcité* (which originally signified the separation of Church and State and the limitation of religion to the private sphere), that are traditionally associated with the left (Reynié, 2011; Camus, 2011). The FN's version was a perversion of *laïcité*, its opponents would say, whereby the legacy of the separation of Church and State in 1905 was adopted to contest the expression of religious diversity in the public space (headscarves, public prayers, ostentatious symbols) and to play more generally to anti-Muslim sentiments in public opinion. More traditional ultra-Catholic sentiment has survived, moreover, and has been articulated powerfully by Marion-Maréchal, J.-M. Le Pen's granddaughter and a former FN deputy (in the southern Vaucluse *département*).

The powerful cocktail of the nation and the people has sustained the FN in France and similar movements elsewhere for several decades. The national reference is pervasive in the FN's repertoire: from the early programmes in favour of national preference onwards, the frame of the nation has been used by the FN to justify otherwise disparate political stances and political messages. In economic policy, for instance, the FN shifted from a position close to radical right economic liberalism and anti-Communism during the 1980s to one of narrow economic protectionism and the protection of workers' rights under Marine Le Pen. Both stances were justified by the register of national protection. During the period under observation, the FN assumed the role of the *parti tribunicien*, the self-styled voice of the people against the elites. In part, this role reflected the electoral base of the FN, which was stronger than any other party in the former industrial heartlands that used to provide mass support for the Parti Communiste Français (PCF, French Communist Party). Rather like national populist parties elsewhere, in 2017 the FN surfed the wave of Euroscepticism, of hostility to 'Brussels' and of fear of the economic crisis. The 2017 electoral series suggested that such a path represented a dead-end. The centrepiece policy of FN policy during the run-up to the 2017 campaign was that of France's exit from the European single currency, or Frexit; coming shortly after the UK's Brexit referendum, the FN's stance sustained a state of apprehension elsewhere and nervousness in world markets.

The period was also marked by the rise of alternative forms of left-wing mobilisation from the turn of the century onwards, of which Jean-Luc Mélenchon's various organisations, the Parti de Gauche (PG, Left Party), the Front de Gauche (Left Front) and LFI have been the main exemplars. There has long been a robust tradition of the far-left in French politics, exemplified by the PCF, France's leading party for much of the post-war Fourth Republic (1946–58) (Pudal, 2004). From an electoral highpoint of 28.6% in 1946, however, the last independent PCF candidate obtained a mere 2% in the 2007 presidential election. In the past two decades, various parties on the anti-system left have performed well, as manifested notably in the strong showing of a variety of Trotskyite candidates in the 1995, 2002 and 2007 presidential elections (De Waele and Seiler, 2012; Pina, 2011). By 2012, most of the political space to the left of the PS was occupied by Mélenchon, a skilful political entrepreneur who left the PS in 2008 and built up the PG as an alternative to the traditional parties of the Union of the Left (the PCF and the PS). Fuelled in part by the fracture over European integration within the left following the 2005 referendum (Escalona and Viera, 2014), Mélenchon provided a practical demonstration of the efficiency of a left-wing alternative in the 2012 campaign, where he polled over 11% in 2012. Mélenchon's stock as an alternative left-wing voice rose with the crisis of the Socialists in office from 2012 to 2017. To understand Mélenchon's success as a political entrepreneur, however, the analyst needs to go beyond structural considerations of political space and performance and acknowledge the skill with which the left-wing politician exploited the personalisation inherent in the French presidency by centring media attention on his leadership and policy programme.

The breakthrough of Mélenchon and his movement is rooted in a broader European movement thriving on the discomfort and rejection of traditional social democracy. This eclectic movement has sometimes taken the form of new organisations (Syriza in Greece, Podemos in Spain); it has sometimes manifested itself within the framework of an existing party (Jeremy Corbyn in the UK Labour Party), or taken the form of social movements beyond party (March and Keith, 2016). Beyond considerations of political space and appeal, Mélenchon's strategy for 2017 was interesting insofar as it involved investing in a loosely bounded movement, not a traditional party organisation. Drawing conclusions from the limits of the PG and the conflictual nature of relationships with the PCF within the Front de Gauche (2012), Mélenchon in turn elided the party form in preparation for the 2017 presidential elections. In the circumstances, this was a good call. It formed part of the process of reframing LFI away from a traditional left-wing party to a movement focused on national protection and anti-imperialist rhetoric, with overtones of nostalgia for the romantic revolutionary movement of Chavism in Venezuela (Marty, 2017; Geai, 2017). The theme of *dégagisme* (literally, blowing away the old system and parties) developed by Mélenchon corresponded to the prevailing ethos.

France is back

Finally, the spring revolution took place in a specific Europeanised and international context, which, though beyond the scope of the work, provided the backdrop to the analysis presented here. Much of the media commentary centred on what might have happened, had France been subjected to a run-off between Le Pen and Mélenchon. The Hollande presidency was widely considered to be one of diminished French capacity at the European level. In the context of Brexit, territorial challenges to the integrity of EU states and boundary- and migration-related issues testing the core of European solidarity, it was a sign of the times that only one candidate – Macron – explicitly engaged himself in defence of the European project, including a public commitment to bring France back within the criteria of the Maastricht Stability Pact. Once installed as president, Macron exploited a favourable set of circumstances to lend leadership credibility to his claim that France is back.

The book

The book is divided into two main parts. Part I, 'Out with the old', focuses mainly on the events of 2016 and 2017, as experienced by key actors of the 'old' world: the then President Hollande, former President Sarkozy and former premier (and 2017 LR candidate) François Fillon. Chapter 1 interprets 2016 as President Hollande's *annus horribilis*: by the end of 2016, Hollande had been forced to abandon any plans he entertained to stand as a candidate for his re-election, the first time this had happened during the Fifth Republic. Chapter 2 considers the political fate of another former president, Nicolas Sarkozy, who was swept aside by the dynamics of the primary election process he had attempted to resist. Chapter 2 also investigates the mechanism of the primary election, in which François Fillon gained the LR nomination by promising economic recovery based on a fundamental overhaul of the French state and public sector and a renewal of France's influence in the world. In Chapter 3, the PS primaries are in turn discussed, and their surprise result – the victory of Benoît Hamon over the incumbent premier, Manuel Valls – dissected. The chapter provides the appropriate space for the obituary of the PS, one of France's hitherto most powerful political parties yet struggling against the odds for its own survival.

In Part II, 'A spring revolution', Chapter 4 considers the 2017 presidential campaign as a very strange affair, where there was no clear presidential front-runner (at least until the centrist François Bayrou stood down in favour of Macron) and no absolute certainty about which candidates would win through to the second round. Chapters 5 and 6 interpret Macron in terms of his political persona, political leadership and global presence, while the Conclusion provides a balanced answer to the question of the transformative nature of the Macron presidency and reflects on the likely future evolution of French and European politics.

Emmanuel Macron was elected as president at a critical juncture in modern French and European history. The new President Macron encountered some early successes in his attempt to restore the prestige of the presidency, domestically, at the European level and in the broader concert of nations. The case of Macron is thereby an exemplary one for testing the possibilities of a national political leadership in a context of declining trust but enhanced interdependence. While awaiting an analysis of Macron's political leadership in the second part of the book, the reader's attention is now drawn to the complex events of 2016–17 that apparently swept away the old world.

Note

1   Debré, 1959–62; Pompidou, 1962–68; Couve de Murville, 1968–69; Chaban-Delmas, 1969–72; Messmer, 1972–74; Chirac, 1974–76; Barre, 1976–81; Mauroy, 1981–84; Fabius, 1984–86; Chirac, 1986–88; Rocard, 1988–91; Cresson, 1991–92; Bérégovoy, 1992–93; Balladur, 1993–95; Juppé, 1995–97; Jospin, 1997–2002; Raffarin, 2002–05; De Villepin, 2005–07; Fillon, 2007–12; Ayrault, 2012–14; Valls, 2014–16; Cazeneuve, 2016–17; Philippe, 2017–.

Part I

Out with the old

1

2016: François Hollande's *annus horribilis*

FRANÇOIS Hollande was elected as France's second Socialist president in May 2012. By his mid-term in office, his presidency had broken all records in terms of unpopularity, and there was a widely diffused public perception of the individual being a poor fit for the accepted institutional role. The key to understanding Hollande's fall lay in the nature of his positioning as a 'normal' candidate and president (see below) and in his actions in the very early days of the presidency. The seventh president of the Fifth Republic exhausted his political resources almost from day one. His behaviour seemed rather reminiscent of that of the Third Republic radical politician Henri Queuille, whose legendary motto was 'it is urgent to wait'. Hollande celebrated his election by taking three weeks' holiday immediately after the election campaign, in an ostensible effort to slow down the presidency.

The consensus view on the first three years of the Hollande presidency was a negative one. The president proved incapable of controlling the divisions within his governments, or of exercising the authoritative behaviour that has come to be expected of French presidents (by dismissing opponents, notably). The president's inability to see off the revolt by the *frondeurs* – with as many as fifty PS deputies willing to vote against the government – was an obvious weakness. More fundamental still was the ambiguity of the political project, sustained – but also undermined – by the radical promises made during his campaign speech at Le Bourget in January 2012. The Hollande presidency became equated with a sense of drift, of weak government and of PS internal dynamics continuing to play themselves out within the government. I have argued elsewhere (Cole, 2014) that there was a psychologically devastating gap between campaign promises and policy platforms on the one hand and actions within government on the other. From early 2015 onwards, however, Hollande experienced a new phase in his presidency, a revival in public opinion against the background of war and terrorist attacks. In early and late 2015, indeed, Hollande appeared as the embodiment of national unity against the internal and external terrorist threat. The right tone was struck, in the mass rallies of 11 January 2015 in defence of the Republic after the attacks on *Charlie-Hebdo* and in the convoking of Congress in Versailles, just days after the 13 November 2015 outrage (the murders at the Bataclan nightclub). At the end of December 2015 Hollande obtained some of his best poll ratings since taking office. In an IFOP–Fiducial poll for *Paris Match* and Sud Radio of 27–8 November 2015, Hollande obtained 50% of positive opinions (cited in *Le Monde*, 2–4 January 2016).

Such a resurrection was short-lived. By 26 April 2016, Hollande was credited with only 17% of favourable opinions (83% were unfavourable) in an Odoxa survey for *L'Express*. 2016 turned out to be President Hollande's *annus horribilis*. The incumbent president's misfortunes in 2016 appeared to be compounded by the quickening pace of political decline as the 2017 presidential election approached. In mid-2016, Hollande appeared to face an impossible dilemma: to be the first president not to stand for re-election, or to stand as candidate with the danger of not reaching the second round. In the third wave of the barometer of the CEVIPOF (Centre pour l'Étude de la Vie Politique Française) in March 2016, for example, by far the largest rolling survey with over 20,000 respondents, Hollande was in third position behind Marine Le Pen and the Republican candidate, whether represented by Alain Juppé (14%) or Nicolas Sarkozy (16%) (IPSOS–CEVIPOF–*Le Monde*, 2016). Hence the incumbent president would be eliminated on the first round. The announcement in December 2016 that he would not be standing for re-election was without precedent in the Fifth Republic, testament to weight of political forces aligned against him.

Hollande's predicament might be interpreted in terms of a series of inappropriate responses to specific events, in which case the Socialist president was a victim of the normal rhythms of extraordinary times. There were any number of key events to choose from: the aborted constitutional reform of 2016 is considered below. Hollande's descent might also be interpreted as the culmination of a series of design faults: the original sin of the mode of election in 2012; the result of a particular style and discourse; the unintended consequences of the political responses to the terrorist attacks of 2015; the longer-term impact of economic crisis and the failure to bring down unemployment. All of these factors recall the weak political, partisan and sociological basis of Hollande's support from the outset. To understand Hollande's predicament we need thereby to mix levels of analysis: to capture the structural, partisan and political bases of his persistent presidential weakness.

Hollande's original sin

Hollande's original sin lay in the manner of his election in 2012. His 2012 presidential campaign was fought in large part as an anti-Sarkozy referendum, designed to preserve an early opinion poll lead that was mainly built upon a popular rejection of Sarkozy. A majority of second-round voters (51%, compared with 31% in 2007) declared that they had voted negatively (for the candidate best placed to prevent the less preferred candidate from being elected), and only a minority declared they had voted positively for their candidate (49%, compared with 69% in 2007) (Jaffré, 2012). Hollande's candidacy was based on his strategic political positioning as a 'normal' candidate and president, a style that he deliberately adopted so as to be the counterpart of the flamboyant Sarkozy. Once elected, however, Hollande experienced a rapid descent from popularity, one much faster and more thorough than that of any previous president. The failure to act during the first 100 days represented a lost opportunity. He was trapped by the frame of normality during a period of economic crisis; the attraction of a 'normal' president who ignored the economic tempest in a wave of enforced optimism soon wore off (Davet and Lhomme, 2016). For the 2012 electoral series was fought in a context of economic crisis; voters were almost as pessimistic about the ability of Hollande to 'improve the situation of the country' (26%) as they were about Sarkozy (25%) (Jaffré, 2012).

There is an argument that normality was an inadequate frame for the French presidency – an exceptional office faced with exceptionally difficult times. Worse, Hollande failed to live up to the norms he had advocated. During the campaign, normality was presented as an ethical standard even more than as a way of conceiving presidential practice. Hollande's claim to normality involved a commitment to keep his private life out of the public domain, but the public jealously displayed by Valérie Trierweiler, his erstwhile partner, destroyed this aspiration very early on. Hollande's personal judgement was then called into question by a succession of scandals involving leading figures of the Socialist-led government (Amar, 2014). By far the most important scandal was that of Jérôme Cahouzec, the budget minister whose reputation for integrity was destroyed by evidence of a secret bank account in Switzerland (despite his repeated denials).

I have argued elsewhere that the Hollande presidency was undermined by the weakness of a consistent legitimising discourse (Cole, 2014). It was unclear to many what Hollande represented. There was a weakness of story-telling, the construction of a coherent narrative to describe and justify governmental action. Was Hollande a traditional social democrat? There was certainly a sustained effort during the Ayrault premiership (2012–14) to revive a social-democratic discourse, and to give substance to this by using social-democratic instruments such as the annual social conference between the government, the business associations and the trade unions; the principle of negotiated solutions to labour laws and training; and the State's involvement in attempting to reduce unemployment by creating subsidised jobs for young people. The core problem lay in the inability to resolve the most intractable policy issue of them all, unemployment. Hollande's commitment in late 2012 to 'reverse' the rising level of unemployment provided a hostage to fortune. By early 2016, however, no major decline of the unemployment rate had occurred, with France comparing unfavourably with its main EU partners and competitors. Hollande did not convince as a social-democratic president, not least because of his inability to resolve this most intractable problem of domestic policy. Was he more successful as a 'social liberal'? Hollande began the 'social liberal' turn in 2013, when the government introduced a tax credit for businesses (*crédit d'impôt pour la compétitivité et l'emploi* or CICE, Tax Credit for Competitiveness and Employment). The CICE laid the basis for the Responsibility Pact announced in January 2014, whereby fifty billion euros of reductions in business taxes were announced, with the expectation that firms would invest and employ more labour (though without any formally constraining conditions). If the social liberal orientation was determined by Hollande's choices, the responsibility for validation lay with Prime Minister Valls (from April 2014) and increasingly with the ambitious economy minister, Macron, who steered his own liberalisation programme in 2015.

As president, Hollande enjoyed the most success with a Republican narrative centred on education, citizenship, the role of France in the international arena and the nation. Even more than his predecessors, Hollande took solace in European and foreign affairs, the traditional 'reserved domain' of the French president (Howorth, 2013). Hollande grew into the role of president in part as war leader: from 2012 to 2017 France intervened in Mali and the Central African Republic and participated in air strikes in Iraq and Syria. The French intervention in Mali in 2013, to dislodge Islamic militants from the north of this strategically important African country and safeguard the capital Bamako, was successful. France was active, if not particularly effective, in Syria and Iraq, from the failed attempt to impose air strikes on Syria's Assad in 2013 to the bombing campaign against so-called Islamic State after the 13 November 2015 Paris massacres. In terms of its soft power, Hollande's team successfully managed a global environment conference, the COP 21, which brought leaders across the world to Paris in December 2015 to pledge their commitments to control global warming and save the planet.

At the European level, Hollande fought his 2012 presidential campaign as a compromise candidate between the various families of the French left; personally strongly pro-European and social democratic, he was deeply conscious of the need to reach out to the *France du non* that had captured a majority of PS voters in the 2005 referendum.[1] His attempts to reorient the EU in a less 'liberal' direction, however, and to assert an alternative, more growth inspired path did not amount to much. Though as candidate Hollande had insisted he would not ratify the Treaty on Stability, Governance and Growth (TSGG) without its fundamental overhaul, this commitment did not survive the first few months of the presidency, the TSGG being ratified by the French parliament on 11 October 2012 (Drake, 2013). Having ratified this key European treaty, France was then treated in a rather indulgent fashion by the European Commission, which revised the country's deficit and debt targets on three occasions (to insist that it meet the Maastricht Stability Pact criteria by 2014, then 2015, and finally by 2017). Hollande was helped by new allies, such as Matteo Renzi's Italy, and above all by the president of the European Central Bank (ECB), Mario Draghi, who declared in 2012 that he would do 'whatever it takes' to defend the euro and began a programme of quantitative easing to keep interest rates low.

Hollande counted some European successes. He was the driving force behind imposing the European Banking Union upon a reluctant Germany. His key aim was to speed up the establishment of the new banking regime, conferring upon the ECB the overall regulatory authority of the euro-zone's banks and allowing ECB support for threatened banks (which might include French ones in due course). Hollande also played an important role in pulling Europe back from the brink in 2015, as he facilitated an agreement that avoided the exclusion of Greece from the euro-zone. Hollande also demonstrated a proactive presence in the international arena, notably in attempting to find a solution to the Ukrainian crisis (launching the so-called G4 process with German Chancellor Angela Merkel, Russian President Vladimir Putin and Ukrainian President Oleksij Poroshenko); this resulted in the 2015 Minsk agreement, which temporarily froze Russia's territorial ambitions in its near neighbourhood.

Towards the end of the Hollande presidency, however, the decline in French influence appeared more manifest than under Sarkozy. The traditionally central Franco-German relationship was undermined by dissensions on economic policy, the growing imbalances between the French and German economies, controversies over fiscal policy (the support from France and Italy for monetary easing put into place by the ECB at the height of the euro crises of 2012 and 2015) and attitudes towards the euro crisis in general and Greece in particular. Then the refugee and migrant crisis appeared to sweep all before it from summer 2015 onwards, combining with terrorist attacks in France, Germany and Belgium to threaten the future of the Schengen zone. Prime Minister Valls's public criticism of Germany's refugee policy as laxist was deeply resented in Berlin. The new French president would have his work cut out to restore trust.

The fall

In his November 2015 address to the Congress, Hollande received a standing ovation. He also made a dual commitment: to reform the 1958 constitution in order to provide a firmer footing for the state of urgency;[2] and to deprive terrorists (initially those with dual nationality, later all French nationals) of French nationality. These two related but distinct articles were imagined in order to provide a firm response to terrorist attacks, but also to embarrass the political right into supporting constitutional reform.

Once the dust of the Versailles speech had settled, the dual offensive was doubly offensive to the 'usual suspects' (the rebel Socialist deputies known as the *frondeurs*, Martine Aubry, the Socialist mayor of Lille, and the 'left of the left' in general), but also more generally to Socialist deputies, if not to broader public opinion (which supported the position adopted by the executive on both counts). The proposal to refer to the state of urgency in the 1958 constitution was criticised by some lawyers as providing a constitutional basis for what is by definition an irregular process (Beaud, 2016), but these arguments left public opinion indifferent. Hollande's manoeuvre was designed to rally support from across the political spectrum, and in particular from the Republicans, whose approval would be necessary to allow any constitutional reform. Here was a potentially popular reform, albeit one that divided constitutionalists, aroused opposition to some of its elements from the Constitutional Council and appeared to strengthen administrative circuits and the police at the expense of legal authority and the judges. Though the state of urgency was not formally included in the constitution, it was renewed on six occasions until finally being rescinded in early November 2017.

The controversy aroused by the state of urgency was as nothing in comparison to that of the proposal to deprive terrorists of their French nationality should they be convicted of terrorist crimes. The initial proposal was to remove French nationality from bi-national citizens born abroad who were convicted of terrorist attacks. In the face of firm opposition, especially from Socialist deputies, an amended proposal was introduced whereby any convicted terrorist could be deprived of their French nationality, potentially creating stateless persons. As Weil (2016) pointed out, there were problems with each of these positions: to deprive only bi-nationals born abroad of their French nationality was tantamount to discrimination and to creating two classes of citizenship (against the equality inherent in the Declarations of the Rights of Man). But the proposal to remove French nationality from any convicted terrorist might leave certain citizens without a nationality. If the first proposal clearly went against the canons of French republican equality, the second one was manifestly contrary to international jurisprudence and law. After four months of high drama, the constitutional reform bill eventually fell in March 2016, Hollande preferring to back down rather than face certain defeat should the measure be presented to the joint houses of parliament meeting as Congress in Versailles (Bekmezian, 2016). The saga alienated the left (including losing the justice minister Christiane Taubira, the symbol of left-wing purity within the Valls government) without rallying the right in support of the change. Eventually both measures fell victim to the decision to abandon the constitutional reform. The real fault was a political one. This idea of removing nationality from terrorists had long been associated with the UMP (Sarkozy supported this position in 2010) and even the FN, whose spokesperson declared the FN's agreement with the proposal. The political damage caused by this saga was considerable for the lack of any positive outcome. The response was to divide further an already emasculated left, without opening up a viable electoral alternative.

One of the core constituencies supporting Hollande in 2012 had been that of the youngest cohorts (aged 18–24 and 25–34). Hard on the heels of the constitutional saga, the proposed El Khomri law revealed how difficult it can be for any government, including a Socialist-led one, to maintain a constructive relationship with youth and young adults (16–24-year-olds) on the verge of entering the labour market. The merits of the El Khomri law, which initially set out to reform (modestly) the labour code and to liberalise (somewhat) the conditions under which firms could lay off workers and to limit job-loss payments, might be debated. The employers' association, the Mouvement des Entreprises de France (MEDEF, Movement of French Firms), had long argued that the French labour code was impossibly complex and posited a clear link between excessive regulation and the refusal of the unemployment curve to begin its movement downwards. In drafting the initial project, Prime Minister Valls listened closely to the MEDEF (and rather less closely to PS deputies or traditional support organisations such as the students' union, the Union Nationale des Étudiants Français). In rather typical style, weak consultation produced a social movement which, in turn, led the government to abandon key elements of the proposed legislation. The proposals that eventually emerged fell far short of their initial ambition. Perhaps the Socialists had nothing to expect from the MEDEF. But the break with youth and young adults was the real downside of this series, even though the most contentious issues were abandoned before the law had been introduced in the Council of Ministers. The mobilisation of students and school pupils against the proposed El Khomri law recalled that a decade earlier against the *Contrat premier emploi* (First Employment Contract) of the Villepin government. The merits of the case need not be reviewed extensively here. The management of the Valls–Hollande tandem was clearly defective. Neither the minister, Myriam El Khomri, nor Prime Minister Valls was able to reassure and satisfy a youth fearful of labour flexibility and desirous of the full-time permanent contracts that their parents enjoyed.

Faced with these setbacks, the opinion surveys published with increasing regularity as the presidential election approached provided little solace for Hollande. The third round of the CEVI-POF's 2017 barometer, in March 2016, cast doubt on Hollande's personal judgement. More recent surveys then suggested that Hollande, as PS candidate, would not reach the second round and, if he did, would be defeated by Marine Le Pen.[3] These findings were extremely damaging, as they undermined Hollande's attempt to position himself as father of the nation, defending the Republic against its enemies. In this *fin de règne* there was new evidence of *lèse majesté*: in the form of the ambitious political positioning of Macron, the new darling of the polls on the left. Though Macron owed his political ascension to President Hollande (he was assistant general secretary of the Élysée, 2012–14, and economy minister from August 2014), in early April 2016 the ambitious *énarque* announced the creation of a new political movement, LRM, explicitly aiming to transcend left and right. This was understandably experienced as a form of treason by Hollande, protector and promoter of the ambitious Macron as a counterweight to Prime Minister Valls and a bridge to the business world. Valls, trapped by solidarity with Hollande and by co-management of the executive for over two years, was no longer the young reformer anxious to sweep aside the existing Socialist order. Macron was much less constrained and more likely to 'kill the father'.

These events told us something about Hollande's presidential style. The official optimism of public speeches throughout the Hollande presidency was in stark contrast with popular perceptions of failure. The 2012–17 presidential term was defined in part by a style that posited a preference for formal consultation over open confrontation. There was much to be said for the art of refined compromise, especially after the fractures of the Sarkozy years. Hollande's celebrated capacity for synthesis was developed over his years as first secretary of the PS, and involved an intimate knowledge of PS networks and of the changing centre of gravity within the party (Raffy, 2011). If the advantage was flexibility and the ability to adapt to a changing centre of gravity, the downside was the challenge of consistency, credibility and coherence. Ultimately, Hollande's reputation suffered from the ambiguities of the 2012 campaign, from the lasting impression of a lack of coordination within the executive and in relations with the Socialist-led majority and, above all, from perceptions of a poor policy record, marked notably by the failure to control unemployment.

The general context that underpins this book is one of strong mistrust in political institutions and political leaders in France. The Hollande presidency did little to dispel such underlying sentiments, and, indeed, the highest recent levels of mistrust were recorded during Hollande's period in office, which was fatally undermined by mistakes and misunderstandings during the first few months. The success of the former president's book *Les leçons du pouvoir* should not obscure the fact that his decision not to stand as a candidate in 2017 was a major humiliation.

Does Hollande's presidency hold lessons for Jeremy Corbyn, the leader of the UK Labour Party and a possible future prime minister? Would the Labour leader also be much heralded when first in office but unable to push through major reforms or make them work? While it is logically impossible to engage in such a counter-factual exercise, the Hollande presidency provided a recent exemplar of the social-democratic dilemma, whereby reformist left parties are forced to operate within the confines of tight economic, European and international constraints and can hope, at best, for a more socially just management of capitalism. The Hollande experience suggests that a Corbyn victory would be the harbinger of more disillusioned days to come.

Notes

1   The phrase *France du non* refers to the small majority of those French electors who turned out to vote which rejected the draft EU constitutional treaty in the 2005 referendum.

2   The state of urgency, ruled by a law dating from 1955 at the height of the Algerian crisis, is not to be confused with the state of emergency (article 16), which allows the president to suspend the normal operation of the constitution.

3   For example, according to the IFOP–Fiducial poll for i-tele, *Paris Match* and Sud Radio (17 April 2016), Le Pen would win a (very hypothetical) Le Pen–Hollande run-off in 2017 by 53% to 47%: www.ifop.com/media/poll/3363-1-study_file.pdf (last accessed 30 August 2017).

2

Bye bye Mr Sarkozy, hello Mr Nobody

THE best-laid plans go astray. In an article written in early November 2016 I was rather surprised that Nicolas Sarkozy, the former President of the French Republic who vowed never to return to politics, seemed to be staring at the possibility of not winning the primary election for the Republican nomination in the 2017 presidential election (Cole, 2016). With the benefit of hindsight, such surprise needs to be substantiated. Why did Sarkozy seem to be a good initial bet? The policy record of the 2007–12 administrations was mixed, and Sarkozy had been soundly defeated in the second round of the 2012 presidential election. But in terms of conquering a party organisation, there appeared to be little doubt. The memory was of Sarkozy as a killer, a bulldozer who would sweep aside all opposition; as the all-conquering former minister who had captured the UMP in 2004 – against opposition from President Chirac – and transformed it into a war machine that swept him to power in the 2007 presidential election; as the comeback kid, who returned from a brief period of crossing the desert (2012–14) and swept aside all challengers to take control of the UMP and transform the party into LR, crowned with electoral success in the departmental and regional elections in 2014–15; as the 'fast president' whose sheer energy was bound to wear down his competitors.

After a couple of years spent crossing the desert (literally, in terms of his involvement in richly remunerated conferences in Qatar), the former president fought back to win control of the UMP in November 2014, renaming the movement Les Républicains.

The change in nomenclature was intended to indicate a shift away from the pretension of the old UMP to be the union of the right and the centre and to create a tougher organisation able to compete with the FN and the Socialists. As one decade earlier, when he had captured control of the UMP, Sarkozy recognised the centrality of party; his main opponents were either unable (Fillon) or uninterested (Juppé) in competing at this level. Controlling the main party – the UMP-turned-Republicans – was intended to act as a trampoline to smooth a trouble-free nomination as the presidential candidate. Sarkozy was well aware of the resources that the control of the main party can bring, such as the definition of the party's platform or the material resources that are available for meetings. He used these resources fully during the period of almost two years at the helm of the LR, before standing down as general secretary with the declaration of his candidacy in late August 2016.

Sarkozy appeared in pole position, but there should have been reasons to doubt: the endless stream of scandals (see below), the ideological compromises, the personal enmities, the challenge of a new generation of ambitious politicians such as Bruno Le Maire all combined to weaken the former president. There was some doubt as to whether Sarkozy would actually be able to stand as a presidential candidate. His judicial worries were never far from the surface, an obstacle vividly recalled by Matthieu Goar in the last week of September 2016. On Monday 26 September, Sarkozy's former chief of police, Bernard Squarcini, was arrested on suspicion of undue influence. On Tuesday 27 September, the blog *Mediapart.fr* produced documentary evidence that again linked the financing of Sarkozy's 2007 campaign with Libya's Colonel Gaddafi (Goar, 2016). On Thursday 29 September, Sarkozy's former guru Patrick Buisson published a damaging account of his years in the Élysée as one of Sarkozy's key advisors (Buisson, 2016); Buisson notably criticised the political insincerity, emotional insecurity and capacity for dirty tricks of his former master. On 30 September, Jean-François Copé, former general secretary of the UMP, published a harsh interview implying that the Bygmalion funding scandal (2012) was entirely due to the incapacity of the 2012 candidate to control campaign expenditure (Goar, 2016). If it was unlikely that these legal worries would come to court before the end of the presidential campaign, they weighed heavily in the background.

The 'open primaries the right and the centre'

The first obstacle to Sarkozy's grand design of re-election as president was that he could not prevent the process of primary elections imposed upon him by two former premiers, Fillon and Juppé. These Republican heavyweights were able, for once, to force Sarkozy to respect party rules. The primaries offered a window for the LR to demonstrate its strength. The deep unpopularity of the incumbent president, François Hollande, and the deleterious state of relations on the left bestowed a vital interest on the Republican primary. The victor of the Republican primary stood a very good chance of being elected the next president, given the state of unpopularity and division on the left and the 'glass ceiling' that was always likely to prevent the FN candidate, Marine Le Pen, from victory, even in the likely event that she reached the second round. Sarkozy had a stronger base in the movement than any of the contenders; he boasted the support of more parliamentarians, party officials, councillors and activists than any of the other primary candidates. There were many grounds to believe in his presidential chances and his success in the LR primary.

The 'open primaries of the right and the centre' (the formal name given to the primary contest), fought over two Sundays in November 2016, challenged two unwritten 'rules' of the French Fifth Republic. The first is the Gaullist one of the direct relationship between the providential leader and the people unmediated by party. In this tradition, the leader emerges naturally to represent the force of history; the party is a presidential rally to organise support for the exceptional leader (Gaffney, 2015; Tenzer, 1998). If we can recognise the Gaullist genealogy of this style in the history of the French right, for a long time French presidents have no longer corresponded to this ideal. The vibrant primary elections revealed a movement that is anything but subordinate. The hollowing of the Gaullist myth is closely associated with a second unwritten rule: that control of a political party produces a natural advantage for a candidate seeking election to the presidency. Mitterrand in 1981, Chirac in 1995 and Sarkozy in 2007 all represented versions of this truism. The introduction of the primary elections, first for the PS in 2006 and 2011 and then for the right and the centre (in fact, LR), laid bare the shifting foundations of presidential power. Capturing control of the party is no longer an adequate gauge of the ability to stand as the party's candidate. On the Socialist left, Martine Aubry controlled the party from 2008, but failed to win the primary and secure the PS nomination in 2011. Likewise, on the mainstream right, Sarkozy returned to take control of the UMP-turned-LR in 2014, but was unable to master the primaries, which were forced upon him by two former premiers, Alain Juppé and François Fillon.

The two rounds of the primary took place on 20 and 27 November 2016. In technical terms, the LR primary was a success. There were over 4,200,000 voters in the first round (some 9% of the total electoral body), a figure that increased somewhat in the second round. Nobody contested the legitimacy of the process, unlike the Fillon–Copé spat for the leadership for the UMP four years earlier. The primary produced a turnover of almost 17,000,000 euros (on the basis of 8,500,000 electors over the two rounds paying two euros each), half of which was available for the successful candidate in the presidential election campaign itself.

Before the first round, the eventual result appeared wide open, with nearly all commentators predicting a victory for either Juppé, Chirac's former prime minister, or Sarkozy, French president from 2007 to 2012. Seven candidates (Sarkozy, Fillon, Juppé, Nathalie Kosciusko-Morizet, Jean-François Copé, Bruno Le Maire and Jean-Frédéric Poisson) qualified for the contest, which was fought over two rounds. Against many expectations, Sarkozy (20.7%) was distanced in the first round of the primary on 20 November 2016, leaving a buoyant Fillon (44.1%) and a chastened Juppé (28.6%) to fight the run-off on 27 November. For the record, the other candidates were each squeezed by the triumvirate in the lead: Kosciusko-Morizet (2.6%) narrowly outperformed Le Maire (2.4%) to win the battle of the forty-somethings. The wooden spoon was reserved for the unfortunate Copé (0.3%), the former UMP general secretary (elected against Fillon for that position in controversial circumstances in 2012), who trailed the Parti Démocrate Chrétien (Christian Democrat Party) candidate, Poisson (1.5%).

Fillon won the LR primary. He was widely praised for a well-prepared campaign, a detailed and serious policy programme and a professional performance during the three television debates between the seven candidates. By surviving as Sarkozy's premier for five years (2007–12), Fillon had demonstrated personal endurance (Raymond, 2013). Though Sarkozy's treatment of his premier (or 'collaborator', as described in 2007) produced lasting tensions, the fact remained that Fillon and Sarkozy had shared control of the State for five years, and the ex-president rallied without hesitation. At the level of programme and ideology, Fillon claimed to have a programme that would create a 'break' with existing social and economic models (a rather similar claim had been made ten years earlier by Sarkozy). He presented his programme as radical, most explicitly during the second-round debate against Juppé. The centre of gravity of the Fillon programme lay in his attention to socio-economic and State reform. The successful candidate advocated strongly the need to reduce the power of the State in the economy, to bring down company taxation, to end the thirty-five-hour week, to weaken social protection, to support business and enterprise, to engage in a radical reform of the labour market (including a thoroughgoing revision of the labour code) and to shed 500,000 jobs in the public sector (*Valeurs actuelles*, 2016; Goar, 2017). In fairness, the leading candidates were arguing over shades of blue. There was a relative cohesion between the economic policy stances of the main candidates, each promising a version of the most economically liberal programme since Chirac's government of 1986–88, an alliance of the Rassemblement pour la République (RPR, Rally for the Republic) and the Union pour la Démocratie Française (UDF,

Union for French Democracy). The debate between the candidates centred on the extent and rhythm of the shrinkage of the public sector (500,000 jobs in the case of Fillon, 250,000 for Juppé) and how far and fast to reduce public expenditure. Both leading candidates agreed on the need to increase the retirement age to sixty-five.

This relative cohesion in relation to economic policy was disrupted by clearly distinctive positions on foreign policy and the controversy over the role of Putin's Russia, which Fillon sought to bring back into the orbit of European diplomacy. A secondary line of cleavage concerned multiculturalism and cultural liberalism. While Juppé positioned himself as a candidate open to the diverse origins of contemporary society and advocated a respect for minorities, Fillon sent out strong identity markers to the provincial Catholic conservative electorate (notably on family issues and adoption), though he refused to be drawn on abortion or gay marriage. As Fillon's campaign descended into the depths of chaos, from late January 2017 onwards, with the revelation by the press of details of his personal life, the LR candidate relied ever more closely on the ultra-conservative group Sens Commun (Common Values) to provide logistical and ideological support for his candidacy (Faye and Goar, 2017). From the outset, Fillon's programme claimed to be tough on Islamic terrorism (Fillon, 2016). It rejected aspects of multiculturalism and espoused an assimilationist ideology not far from that of Sarkozy. The convergences between Sarkozy and Fillon (strengthened by the rallying of the former to the latter) were demonstrated by the controversy over Fillon's proposals to rewrite history programmes in schools to encourage a 'national narrative'.

In the French context, Fillon's cocktail of economic liberalism and social conservatism raised immediate comparisons with Margaret Thatcher, which were willingly embraced by the LR candidate himself. The LR candidate appeared for a while to occupy the central position in a political landscape marked by a shift to the political right (demonstrated in numerous surveys and notably the CEVIPOF–IPSOS–Sopra Steria 2017 election survey published in *Le Monde*). But this explicit mix of economic liberalism and social conservatism was responsible for the first major decline in public support in January 2017. The French were not ready for a harsh cure of state retrenchment and cuts in public services.

Fillon: the road to hell

The polls carried out immediately after Fillon's election pointed to a comfortable second-round victory for the LR candidate against Marine Le Pen, so much so that the right-wing journal *Valeurs actuelles* announced that he was 'already president' (*Valeurs actuelles*, 2016). But being installed as favourite this far in advance was a mixed blessing – as Juppé had already discovered to his cost in the 'primary of the right and the centre'. Fillon was indeed elected as the LR candidate, but the fall from grace was brutal and rapid. A series of revelations by the satirical newspaper *Le canard enchaîné*, starting on 25 January 2017, revealed that Fillon had employed his wife as a very well-paid parliamentary assistant (since 1981), as well as his children, though they were students at the time. The Fillon scandal (euphemistically known as an 'affair' in French) dominated the campaign. Fillon's ratings plummeted from a high of 28% immediately after the primary to a low of 18% in the weeks before the first round. The substance of the scandal was taken to symbolise changing standards of public behaviour and to focus attention on the question of the conflict of interests. Fillon's reaction of ignoring his initial promise not to stand as candidate if formally investigated by the judiciary made matters worse.

Bye Bye Mr Sarkozy

Fillon's success in obtaining the LR nomination ended the careers of two legends of French politics: Juppé, representing the liberal-conservative wing of LR, and Sarkozy. The second unanticipated result of the first round lay in the counter-performance of Juppé

(28.6%), the former premier and mayor of Bordeaux representing centre-right opinion within LR, who had appeared withdrawn (even complacent) throughout the campaign and who clearly expected to be present, in a commanding position, on the second round against a damaged Sarkozy. Juppé suffered from his open advocacy of the alliance of the right and the centre. Sarkozy hit the mark for a fraction of the LR electorate when he attacked Juppé, on the basis that he would probably ally himself with the centrist Bayrou. Juppé's espousal of general happiness (*l'identité heureuse*) and pleas in favour of multicultural tolerance were notable virtues, but went against the spirit of the times in the ranks of the conservative electorate (Dive, 2016). Was Juppé damaged by the 'Socialists' who openly declared they would vote for him were he to be the candidate? Quite possibly. In the primary, Juppé came runner-up in most regions except for the south-west (six of the twelve *départements* of the Nouvelle Aquitaine region, the zone of influence of Bordeaux), along with a stronger performance in Paris region, where the Île-de-France regional leader Valérie Pecresse had rallied to him.

At least Juppé won through to the second round, which was beyond Sarkozy, who managed to poll just 20.7%, producing an abrupt and immediate end to his political career and making a resurrection unlikely. As the primary campaign unfolded, things did not go exactly to plan for the former president. True, no-one could doubt his energy or the enthusiasm of his supporters. Trailing Juppé in the various opinion surveys carried out over the summer of 2016, Sarkozy had the opportunity during the primary campaign to impose his political leadership and policy choices on the other candidates and rally the Republican base in support of his energetic candidacy. In contrast, the other leading contenders – the front-runner Juppé and the former premier Fillon – attracted less media attention and were strangely absent during key moments. The spate of terrorist attacks during the summer of 2016 (in Nice and St Étienne de Rouvray) seemingly played to Sarkozy's agenda; the former president occupied the media limelight during this vital period. Fuelled by a campaign based on values and identity, Sarkozy began chipping away at

Juppé's initially strong lead in the primary polls (de Montvalon, 2016).

But there were an impressive number of obstacles that combined to prevent the former president from winning the primary. Sarkozy's ideological positioning was one. The secret of Sarkozy's successful 2007 presidential campaign had lain in his capacity to transcend traditional debates between left and right and to accompany the debates over values with precise positions in the field of society, economy and welfare. The period immediately following his election was that of the France of all the talents, the opening-up to the left and civil society actors and the promotion of the new generation of black and North African-origin politicians such as Rachida Dati and Rama Yade. In 2012, on the other hand, Sarkozy was defeated in the second round of the presidential election on the basis of a much narrower programme of values and national identity, the strategy that he adopted again for 2017. To be fair, the linking of immigration and insecurity represented a fairly consistent strand of his political trajectory: his role as a tough interior minister under the prime ministers Raffarin (2002–04) and Villepin (2005–07), the creation of the ephemeral Ministry of Immigration and National Identity in 2007, and the infamous Grenoble speech of 2010, which marked the beginning of a much harsher position on issues of immigration, migration and security, were all testament to this. The early campaign for the Republican primaries (which prefigured an eventual Sarkozy campaign) was dominated by identity-focused debates over the 'Burkhini',[1] special diets in schools, the wearing of Muslim veils in universities and provocations about national origins designed to challenge the desire to assimilate into the national community by those with diverse ethnic, especially Muslim, origins. In a controversial speech in September, Sarkozy remarked that 'the Gauls are our ancestors' and that anybody who contests this should have no place in France (*Le Figaro*, 2016).

The game was a dangerous one. Sarkozy's identity-focused campaign was aimed at siphoning potential FN voters but ignored core socio-economic concerns. Beyond the debate on political positioning lay the questions of the sincerity of Sarkozy's ideological positioning. One policy in particular exemplified this instrumental use of ideology: though responsible as president for the important Grenelle environmental agreements of 2008, by 2016 Sarkozy was calling into question human responsibility for global warming.

In conclusion, Sarkozy appeared increasingly as a general fighting the last war. He played to the hard-core Republican electorate that – he calculated – would be most likely to vote in the primary election. But he appeared less well prepared than the former premier Fillon, and less convincing on grounds of economic liberalisation and state reform than his rival. The 'Duracell president' was finally winding down. His attempts to play the victimisation card rebounded against Sarkozy this time round, his personal credibility called into question by a string of scandals.[2] Strategically, the primaries rewrote the rules of the game and undermined more traditional beliefs in the importance of controlling the party organisation, especially in the context of a deep distrust with political parties. Sarkozy targeted the core LR electorate – but Fillon was more convincing, until dragged down by personal scandal.

Sarkozy stands as one of the most influential politicians of his time, a reformer who energised the French presidency, but whose reforms have not really stood the test of time, with some exceptions. Will he be remembered as the tax-cutting president who raised the fiscal burden over the course of his presidency? As the economic liberal who turned to state intervention? As the friend of diversity who ended up excluding those who challenged the quasi-colonialist belief of 'our ancestors the Gauls'? As the campaign gathered pace, Sarkozy appeared as a 'has been', as did Juppé, the former premier whose welfare reforms had brought the country to a standstill in 1995.

Above all, the fate of Sarkozy gave an early indication of the wide-scale rejection in 2017 of the old – both parties and politicians – who had outstayed their welcome. The UMP-turned-LR was typical of the parties deep in crisis in the period 2012–17. Its name had been blackened by episode of the deeply contested and possibly fraudulent leadership campaign, when J.-F. Copé appeared to have pipped Fillon in the leadership in 2012 by dishonest means (Haegel, 2013). Sarkozy's return was popular amongst hard-core LR party activists, but was indelibly associated with the movement he had built and hoped to revive. In the event, the former president suffered from the general rejection of existing elites that seemed to overwhelm the political class during the spring of 2017.

Notes

1   The Burkhini is a Muslim swimsuit that covers the entire body. In the wake of the Nice attacks on 14 July 2016, several Republican mayors adopted municipal decrees forbidding the wearing of these outfits on France's beaches. These municipal decrees were ruled unlawful by the Council of State.

2   The term 'affair' can have a double meaning in English. The term is used to refer to perceived misdemeanours of a legal or ethical nature, sometimes characterised as political scandals. It is also used in English to apply to incidences of a sexual or relational character. In order to avoid confusion, the book uses the term 'scandal', though this is not exempt from ambiguities.

3

The Socialists in search of survival

THIS chapter, on the fortunes of the French Socialists, is written at two levels of analysis. First, from the narrow perspective of the 2017 presidential competition, it considers the PS primary and the historic defeat of the PS candidate Benoît Hamon in that years's election. More broadly, the chapter discusses the decline and possible demise of the party once described as the natural party of government.

The Parti Socialiste primaries and the Belle Alliance Populaire

In the previous chapter, I argued that the generalisation of the mechanism of primaries to select presidential candidates challenged an unwritten rule of party competition: that control of a political party produces a natural advantage for a candidate seeking election to the presidency. In the case of the Socialists, the success of the PS primaries in 2011 occurred because the voting constituency was broadened well beyond the traditional party members and activists; the party itself was fairly marginal to the procedure and reconfigured on the basis of the results in the primary election (Lefebvre, 2011).[1] Herein lay a paradox: while in 2011 the primary election produced victory for the candidate best placed to defeat the incumbent President Sarkozy, in 2017 the Socialist primaries turned in favour of a candidate – Hamon – who was considered to have no chance whatsoever to win the presidency or even go through to the second round, but who represented a form of ideological purity valued by activists and supporters after five years of compromises in office. The paradox was more apparent than real; in Socialist parties across Europe (the Labour Party in the UK, the Partito Democratico in Italy, the Partido Socialista Obrero Español in Spain), primary elections (or similar mechanisms) have mobilised, first and foremost, enthusiastic (young) activists and sympathisers in search of ideological renewal and survival. In the specific case of the French Socialist primaries, some 73% declared their priority to be that of selecting a candidate faithful to the values of the left, as against only 24% who considered that their vote would help to select a future president (ELABE–BFM, 2017).

If the Socialist primaries were the great innovation of 2011, paving the way for the eventual electoral victory of Hollande in 2012, the primaries of the Belle Alliance Populaire (Great Popular Alliance) which took place on 22 and 29 January 2017 were a pale imitation, a mere side-show to the shaping-up of the presidential contest between the main players: Fillon (LR), Le Pen (FN), Mélenchon (LFI) and Macron (LRM). The polls (for example the CEVIPOF–IPSOS–Sopra Steria survey published in *Le Monde* on 20 January 2017) suggested that the winner of the Socialist primaries – whether Hamon or Valls – would be likely to feature in fifth position in the polls, behind the four aforementioned candidates.

The primaries of the Belle Alliance Populaire were originally conceived as a political instrument to allow incumbent President Hollande to gain momentum and stand for re-election. Hollande's announcement in December 2016 that he would not stand for his own re-election was another novel precedent in the Fifth Republic. Diminished for years as a result of persistently negative opinion polls ratings, Hollande fell victim in part to his proximity to journalists. How else to explain the fact that various confidential state secrets were revealed by two *Le Monde* journalists (Davet and Lhomme, 2016) in a book which did much to damage further Hollande's reputation? The *coup de grâce* was exercised by two former protégés: the former economy minister

Macron, who resigned as minister in summer 2016 to concentrate on creating the LRM movement and standing for the presidency; and the former premier Manuel Valls, who put maximum pressure on Hollande not to stand and to pave the way for his own presidential bid.

The Belle Alliance Populaire had been created with a view to broadening participation in the primary beyond the PS. The three leading candidates were all leading personalities of the Hollande years. Valls, premier from 2014 to 2016, was forced into the role of defender of the record of the 2012–17 governments, which was indefensible in the eyes of the other leading candidates, Hamon and Montebourg. Valls (31.19% on 22 January) had a difficult campaign: beyond the empty venues and frosty receptions, the former premier was forced to fight on the defence of the 2014–16 record in office. He positioned himself as unifier of the left, though he had diagnosed the irreconcilable nature of the two lefts within the PS while still prime minister and called for the replacement of the PS with a more explicitly reformist party back in 2008. The hard line taken on issues of *laïcité* and security was reassuring to some, but deeply hostile to others. The results of the first round, in which Valls (31.19%) trailed Hamon (36.21%), and his eventual defeat on the second round, suggested that the record of the Socialist governments from 2012 to 2017 had become a millstone around the neck of Hollande's longest-serving premier. Valls eventually followed his erstwhile rival Macron into LRM in the June 2017 parliamentary election.

Of the two left candidates, Arnaud Montebourg (17.62%) fought a strangely backward-looking campaign, based on national protectionism, industrial revival ('Made in France') and Keynesian relaunch, which appealed to some traditional PS voters but appeared out of step with the younger, environmentally conscious activists. Hamon (36.21% on 22 January) emerged as the only candidate with a real campaign dynamic, diffused by original ideas on political ecology, social protection (the 'universal revenue'), social liberalisation (the legislation of cannabis, a new visa regime for refugees), constitutional reform (the suppression of article 16 of the 1958 constitution, the eventual creation of a Sixth Republic) and European relaunch (the 'renegotiation' of the Fiscal Compact Treaty (the TSGG), and the renunciation of all debt contracted since 2008). Hamon's campaign gathered momentum explicitly on the promise to revive a Socialist vision and programme. Rather like that of Jeremy Corbyn in the UK, Hamon's appeal lay with those (often very young) supporters and activists who were engaged in re-thinking the future of a progressive left party to be built on the basic foundations of the PS. For the record, the other candidates in the primary were the former education minister, the Socialist Vincent Peillon (6.83%); Sylvie Pinel of the Parti des Radicaux de Gauche (PRG, Party of Left Radicals: 1.99%) and the independent ecologists François de Rugy (3.88%) and Jean-Luc Benhamais (1.01%).

Hamon's score at the presidential election – 6.36% – was worse than even the darkest predictions. The PS barely performed better in the ensuing parliamentary election (7.5% without the support of its small allies) and was reduced to a rump of thirty seats. Hamon's decision to leave the PS after his defeat in the 2017 parliamentary elections and create a new movement (first labelled Mouvement du 1 Juillet, then re-baptised Generation.s) might be interpreted as an act of disloyalty. He was not alone in this respect, however, as the existing parties proved incapable of retaining their most dynamic elements. Hamon's preference for renovating the left from outside the existing party made sense to many of his supporters and underlined the extent of the crisis hitting the PS.

The Socialist primaries were a rather melancholic retrospective on the inability of the French Socialists to reconcile their core contradictions that has a long history. The primary played out, in miniature, the drama that undermined the Socialists throughout the five years of the Hollande presidency, as it set governmental against radical left. The PS demonstrated once again the structural difficulty it has had in accepting the exercise of power. Herein lay the enigma of the party of Épinay, whose decline is now addressed.

The end of the Épinay cycle: lessons from the collapse of the Parti Socialiste

The phrase 'the end of the Épinay cycle' refers to the decline and possible disappearance of the PS, which had been captured by François Mitterrand at the Épinay congress in 1971. The continent-wide crisis of social democracy has been discussed in the Introduction. The decline of the Greek Panellínio Sosialistikó Kínima (PASOK, Panhellenic Socialist Movement) from over 40% to 5% in the course of a few years serves as a permanent reminder of the fragility of the governmental left, as does the inability of the Spanish Partido Socialista Obrero Español to form a government in 2016, as well as the further decline of the German Social Democrats in the 2017 election and the Partito Democratico in Italy in 2018. The French Socialists crystallise these trends. They lost the core material bases of their organisational power during the 2012–17 period, after defeats in the 2014 municipal elections and the 2015 departmental and regional elections and their decimation (to thirty deputies) in the June 2017 parliamentary election. There appears little prospect of a way back from the brink, in contrast with the situation following the calamitous 1993 legislative elections, when the PS, though reduced to sixty-seven deputies, climbed back to win office four years later.

Mitterrand's conquest, mastery and subjugation of the PS during the decade after the congress of Épinay in 1971 was the major political occurrence of the 1970s. The post-1971 PS represented, amongst other things, an uneasy compromise between a Gaullien-style presidential rally (inspired by Mitterrand's leadership after 1971) and a strong tradition of party organisation and self-sufficiency (as embodied in the old Section Française de l'Internationale Ouvrière, or SFIO, the French Section of the Workers' International). The post-1971 party laid great stress on its quality as an activists' party (*parti de militants*), a democratic party, an aspiring mass party and a movement inspired by the ideals of May 1968 (Barboni, 2009; Olivier, 2009). The other face of the party was as an efficient electoral machine, especially in local and regional elections and on occasion in relation to the key presidential contest as well. In the ensuing section, four principal claims to historical significance of the post-1971 PS are identified which contributed to the party's success; by late 2016, each of these distinctive characteristics had become untenable or unconvincing.

The first claim to historical significance was as the people's party. Part of the obsession of the French Socialists with the PCF was sociological; that the PCF attracted the bulk of working-class left-wing support from 1936 onwards gave the PS (then known as the SFIO) a perpetual ideological inferiority complex vis-à-vis the Communists (Portelli, 1980). The SFIO, in the Fourth and early Fifth Republics, represented a stable electorate of lower civil servants, office employees and public-sector workers, but failed to penetrate the industrial working class, except in areas of northern France. One of the major shifts of the 1970s was the transformation of the PS (which replaced the SFIO in 1969) into, first, a popular, and, second, an inter-class party. The strategy of its United Left alliance (PS, PCF, PRG) was dictated in part by instrumental electoral considerations: namely how to attract the support of five million mainly working-class Communist electors, as Mitterrand publicly boasted was his aim in 1972. By 1978 the PS drew almost as much support from industrial workers as the PCF, and by 1981 the PS candidate Mitterrand had overtaken the PCF's Marchais (Capdevielle, 1981; Schweisguth, 1983). On a sociological level, the PS (in 1981 and 1988 especially) appeared to be a genuinely inter-class party, repeating a feat achieved previously only by the Gaullists in the 1960s.

The electoral coalitions built by Mitterrand in 1981 and 1988 were not sufficiently robust to guarantee against a downturn in party fortunes after the inevitable compromises made in office. In 1993, the party lost almost half of its 1988 electorate, and, though the decline from the 1997 election was less marked in 2002, the direction was the same. In 1993 and 2002, the popular electorate in particular lost faith in the Socialists after long periods in office. This established a pattern in successive elections of strong support amongst higher-management and public-sector cadres, but a weak presence amongst industrial workers and employees, a phenomenon that bears some similarities with the Labour Party's loss of traditional working-class support in the UK (Lefebvre and Sawicki, 2007; Escalona, 2017).

The second claim to historical significance was as a broad church of progressive forces on the centre and left of French politics. The revival of the PS during the 1970s was linked in part to its capacity to mobilise the new social movements galvanised by May 1968 (ecologists, students, feminists, regionalists, anti-racist and alternative left groups) as well as the party's credibility as a pole of attraction for existing groups – such as the Parti Socialiste Unifié (United Socialist Party) – that had refused to join the old SFIO. The combination of social movement and new political activists created a dynamic Socialist eco-system, with the party at the centre of theoretical innovations and social experiments. To retain such a broad church within the party, the PS adapted its party rules, notably by using a system of proportional election (PR) for internal party elections, whereby factions, or 'currents', were officially represented in the party's representative parliament (*bureau national*). Beyond organisational incentives, the leading factions within the PS each either represented specific political traditions (the self-identified left, reformist and municipal factions, for example) or held strongholds within the party itself (such as the party organisation, the parliamentary party, local government or think tanks) or some combination of these.

Analysis of party factionalism lies beyond the scope of this chapter (Cole, 1989). During the heady years of expansion, internal diversity was valued as a positive democratic quality. In politically less favourable periods, however, factionalism was experienced as divisive and debilitating. The organisational history of the PS's demise, culminating in 2017, was one of the hollowing-out of the party's orthodox centre, undermined by new political cleavages (over Europe and the economy, notably) and, especially, by the revival of party factionalism during the Hollande presidency, in the form of the *frondeurs* (the name given to the thirty to fifty rebellious PS deputies), best understood as the most recent manifestation of the left faction within French Socialism.[2]

The third claim to historical significance was that of being the presidential party or, at least, the only party on the left which could credibly claim to win a presidential election, a feat its candidate achieved in 1981 and 2012. On both occasions of Socialist victory, however, there was a lively tension between party traditions of self-sufficiency and autonomy and the executive-centred equilibrium of the Fifth Republic. Upon his election in 1981, Mitterrand made it clear that the majority 'presidential' party would be subordinate to the popularly elected president and his government. In his first message to Socialist deputies, the new president insisted that the '110 propositions' were 'the charter of the government's activity, and therefore of your legislative programme' (Charlot, 1983). Even under Mitterrand, the PS had difficulties in accepting such a subordinate role. Opposition was strongest from amongst the left faction, the Centre d'Études et de Recherches Socialistes (CERES, Centre for Socialist Studies and Research), whose leader, Jean-Pierre Chevènement, resigned from government twice in protest. In 2012, Hollande presided over an almost total collapse of the presidential party. The formal mechanism functioned: an overall PS majority was returned on the coat-tails of the presidential victory in 2012. From the outset, however, the existence of the well-organised left faction – the *frondeurs* – undermined the overall cohesion of the governmental machine and divided the PS parliamentary group, which became a powerful source of resistance to the Ayrault and Valls govern-ments. The withering-away of the presidential party was particularly acute in the case of the French Socialists, but is a more general phenomenon in the Fifth Republic, as tensions between the personalisation of the presidential institutions confront the myriad of political ambitions present amongst elected deputies.

Finally, the most solid claim to significance maintained by the French Socialists was as a territorial party, well rooted in local and regional government. The new PS grew fastest during the 1970s in areas of traditional SFIO weakness, such as Brittany. The Socialists' victories in the 1977 municipal elections across France further diversified the structures of local Socialist power and influence within the party. Indeed, the party's most dynamic factions recruited outside the traditional party strongholds and relied often on the conquest of new strongholds in local government. As the party's fortunes declined in national elections after 1993, so the weight of its local and regional elected officials grew. From 2004 to 2014, the PS controlled the vast majority of elected regions (twenty out of twenty-two) and a majority of *départements* and large cities. With electoral success, new structures became influential within the party, such as the Association des Régions de France (Regional Council Association), which was strongly supportive of Royal's candidacy in 2006.

The PS might also be described as a municipal party in a rather more pejorative sense, in that there was little consistency between positions adopted at the national or the local level. One measure of Mitterrand's control over the PS in the 1970s lay in the decision to impose United Left lists in all towns of over 30,000 inhabitants, to the extent of expelling diehard resisters. By 1977, with the Union of the Left strategy firmly in place, the party leadership managed to impose United Left lists almost everywhere, and expelled recalcitrants. By 1983, even the traditionally anti-Communist Gaston Defferre had accepted a United Left list in Marseille. By 2001, however, powerful incumbent mayors began to distance themselves from central requirements. By 2008 and 2014, the wheel had almost turned full circle as local alliances depended mainly on local situations. Powerful figures such as Gérard Collomb, mayor of Lyon since 2001, were simply not prepared to conform to central guidance about the composition of local party lists.

The territorial party has resisted rather better than the other emanations. In 2017, Macron managed to rally the support of key PS local and regional government figures, such as Jean-Yves Le Drian (president of the Brittany region, foreign affairs minister under Philippe) and Collomb (who also served as interior minister under Philippe), as well as forty-nine incumbent deputies. But the 2017 Senatorial elections demonstrated a new spirit of resistance amongst the remaining PS *élus*. The future challenge for LRM, in the 2020 municipal elections, will be to replicate its national success on the local level; the precedent of the Gaullist

Union pour la Nouvelle République (UNR, Union for the New Republic) – which, though dominant nationally, initially performed poorly in local elections – is scarcely encouraging in this respect, which gives some hope to the Socialists that more clement days might lie ahead.

In his book *When Political Parties Die*, Mack (2010) presents a model of the collapse of major parties of government. Such parties include the mid-nineteenth-century US Whig Party (replaced by the Republican Party after being incapable of reaching internal agreement on the issues of slavery and immigration), the British Liberal Party (overtaken by the Labour Party in the 1920s) and Canada's now forgotten Progressive Conservative Party (which collapsed in 1993). Other examples would include the French Parti Radical (Radical Party) or more recent cases such as the Greek PASOK. Mack identifies three major causal explanations: the loss of credibility with the core electoral base (the electoral dimension); the existence of party alternatives (the partisan competitor dimension); and the blurring or betraying of party principles (the ideological dimension). Once this explosive cocktail is established, the party loses credibility (Escalona, 2017). In the case of the Socialists, there had been a long-term decline of the electoral base, but this movement gathered speed after the 2015 regional election, the last election in which the PS performed credibly (it still runs five of the twelve mainland French regions). Not only was 2016 Hollande's *annus horribilis* (see Chapter 1), but it also represented a watershed, as PS electors, activists and politicians were deeply divided over government policy, specifically the nationality and labour market reforms. From 2016 onwards, there were rival competitors, in the form of Mélenchon's LFI and, above all, Macron's LRM (whose programme was well received by core PS electors in the higher managerial and professional categories). The end of the Épinay cycle probably signifies the end of the PS itself, at least in the form recreated in 1971, with the party's decline involving an explosive mix of the four core dimensions surveyed above: sociological change (the loss of, first, the popular and, second, the professional and managerial electorate), organisational challenges (the divisive impact of internal factionalism), a poor institutional fit (the unresolved relationship between the party and the presidential institutions) and profound policy disagreements (played out through the 2012–17 governments in the division between the governmental and radical left). Only the territorial dimension of the PS machine remained – for the moment – largely intact. There are few examples of a party bouncing back. If it is still somewhat premature to write the final epitaph, the chapter now concludes with a melancholic epilogue.

Epilogue

One year after the PS primaries, not much remained of the party created in 1905 and revived at Épinay in 1971. The parliamentary election of June 2017 witnessed a virtually total collapse of the PS, which was reduced to a rump of thirty deputies. The party's historic headquarters at the rue de Solferino was being sold; and the rump parliamentary party changed its name to the Nouvelle Gauche (New Left). The first immediate casualty was a crisis of leadership, with the resignation of Jean-Christophe Cambedelis after the electoral collapse and creation of a transitory collective leadership. A fight for control of the party ensued; it was resolved in favour of Olivier Faure, the former leader of the Socialist deputies, who defeated his rivals Stéphane Le Foll, Emmanuel Maurel and Luc Carvounhas in an internal vote of the 100,000 remaining party members. However, former President Hollande refused to retire with dignity and insisted on performing the role of elephant in the room, producing a best-seller (*Les leçons du pouvoir*, published by Stock of Paris in 2018) and occupying the media limelight. Hollande's schadenfreude proved of little succour to the new PS leader Faure.

More than ever, the party organisation was too weak to control the operation of currents: either those now external to the party, as in the case of Hamon's movement Generation.s, or new ginger groups created by prominent personalities, such as Mayor Annie Hidalgo in Paris. There was a shift to the remaining mayors of large cities. But the PS remained also very vulnerable to the continuing pull of Macron, as illustrated by the case of Olivier Dussopt, mayor of Annonay and one of the few young PS deputies to be re-elected, deserting to the Macron camp in early 2018. One PS deputy, interviewed in May 2018, went so far as to declare that the future of the PS 'lies entirely in Macron's hands', with future defections likely. On the left, the rump PS is squeezed by the performance of Mélenchon and the attractiveness of his LFI movement. If the honourable resistance in the 2017 Senatorial elections demonstrated that it is too early to bury the PS, the party appears as the most prominent victim of the crisis of trust in established political parties, and in an even more desperate situation than LR.

Notes

1   In 2011 and 2017, the PS primary invited all supporters to participate in the process of candidate selection upon payment of a modest fee, while in 2006 this right had been reserved to party members.

2   The left faction has been a constant in the history of French Socialism. Already, in the 1930s, left factions had formed in opposition to Blum and the Front Populaire (Popular Front). In the 1960s, Jean Poperen's Bataille Socialiste (Socialist Struggle) challenged the control of the party by Guy Mollet. In the 1970s, the CERES was a tightly organised parallel faction which sought to capture the party from the left. CERES eventually left the party (the historic leader Chevènement creating the Mouvement des Citoyens, or Citizens' Movement, in 1991). The left opposition mantle then passed to Jean-Luc Mélenchon, minister in Jospin's 1997–2002 government, who also left the PS in 2008 to create the PG. The *frondeurs* were the latest in a long tradition.

Part II

A spring revolution

4

Of volcanoes and earthquakes: looking back at the 2017 presidential and parliamentary elections

IF the 2002 presidential election was a strange affair, the 2017 contest turned out to be even stranger. Between the two elections, the electoral scenarios shifted. In 2002, Jean-Marie Le Pen won through to the second round against expectations, with almost 18% in the first round; massive Republican mobilisation saw the incumbent President Jacques Chirac re-elected with a large majority (81.75%). In 2017, few commentators cast any doubt on the likely presence of Marine Le Pen in the second round, though predictions of a Le Pen victory were more prevalent in the foreign media than amongst French commentators. While the expectation that a left–right cleavage will produce a run-off between a Socialist and a Republican candidate has underpinned most presidential elections, such a scenario appeared most unlikely in 2017 and, indeed, did not materialise. But it was difficult to keep tabs on this campaign, and several scenarios remained open until the first ballot on 23 April 2017. There appeared for a long time to be no presidential front-runner and no absolute certainty about which candidates would win through to the second round. As it evolved, an increasingly likely scenario was that of a run-off between two candidates portraying themselves as anti-system: Marine Le Pen for the FN and Emmanuel Macron of LRM. Both candidates successfully positioned themselves as above party; somewhat paradoxically, the absence of primary elections in the case of these two candidates strengthened their claim not to be dependent on party.

In terms of the campaign proper, 2017 was marked by the rise and fall of individual candidates: the LR candidate descended rapidly from his post-primary pedestal as the Fillon scandal gripped the public's attention (28% of forecast votes in November 2016; 24% in January 2016 before the 'affair' broke; 18% at the height of the crisis). Le Pen started with a commanding lead, surfing on the FN's status as the leading party of France in the three previous elections (the European elections of 2014, the departmental elections of 2015 and the regional elections of 2015). As Table 4.1 illustrates, her lead narrowed throughout the campaign; inaudible (by choice) until early February, as a consequence of her quest for respectability, she started campaigning in earnest at around the same time as the scandal over FN assistants in the European parliament deepened.[1] By the time Hamon secured the PS nomination, in February 2017, the campaign had only a couple of months left to run (and the first month was wasted in negotiations with Europe Écologie les Verts (EELV, Europe, Ecology, the Greens) and Mélenchon's LFI). The two most successful first-round candidates were Mélenchon, who rose from 9% to almost 20% over the course the campaign, and Macron of LRM, whose faltering campaign was decisively boosted by the decision of François Bayrou, the historic centrist, not to stand as candidate and his rallying to Macron in February 2017.

Looking back

The 2017 campaign rewrote almost all of the rules and presuppositions associated with the presidential election. French presidential elections are usually fought in the context of the record of an outgoing government and an election campaign. For the first time in the Fifth Republic, the incumbent president decided not to stand for re-election, thereby depriving the campaign of one of its major political functions (testing the accountability of an outgoing administration). Following the defeat of Valls in the Socialist primary, no single candidate in the 2017

Table 4.1 Campaign fortunes of the leading candidates in 2017

Candidate	Percentage of votes							
	Jan 2016	May 2016	Sept 2016	Dec 2016	Feb 2017	April 2017	Result, 23 April 2017
Marine Le Pen	26	28	29	24	26	22.5	21.3
PS candidate (Hollande, Valls/Hamon)	20	14	13	11	14.5	8	6.36
LR candidate (Sarkozy/Fillon)	21	21	22	26	18.5	19.5	20.01
Mélenchon	9	12	13	13	12	19	19.58
Macron	–	–	–	13	23	23	24.01
Bayrou	13	13	12	6	–	–	–

Source: Figures drawn from the CEVIPOF–IPSOS–Sopra Steria *Enquête électorale française* (see note 2). The 23 April 2017 figure is that provided by the French Interior Ministry.

campaign explicitly defended the record of the outgoing government, in part as a consequence of the primary elections.

The primaries presented a paradoxical mix of challenges and
opportunities for the existing parties. To recall, the 'open primaries
of the right and the centre' were contested in November 2016,
while the PS and the PRG (in the Belle Alliance Populaire) held
their internal primaries in January 2017. Each primary campaign
produced an early promise based on the premises of a clear
victor. In the case of the LR primary, most observers had assumed
that the run-off would pit Sarkozy against the former premier
Juppé. In the event, Fillon, long considered as the outsider,
emerged in powerful first position (44.1%), though he had been
trailing in fourth place with barely 10% a few weeks earlier. The
Socialist primary was held two months later and again produced
an upset, as the third-placed candidate Hamon came from behind
to eliminate his fellow *frondeur* Montebourg on the first round
before defeating the former premier Valls on the run-off (56.69%
to Valls's 41.31%). The tone was set for the most unpredictable
of election campaigns.

The logic of the primaries extended far beyond the selection
of the party's candidate. At the height of the Fillon scandal in
early March 2017, the Republican candidate used the result of
the LR primaries to fend off challenges to his candidacy. As Fillon
pointed out, in a televised interview on France 2 (5 March 2017),
no-one could prevent him from standing as candidate (all the
more in that he had already deposited the 500 signatories necessary to stand), not even the investigating magistrates who
announced the opening of a legal enquiry and ordered the
candidate to appear before them on 15 March. On the Socialist
left, the lasting impact of the primary was to create a gulf between
the candidate and the mass of PS deputies, who were deeply
anxious about their – slim – prospects of re-election with the
PS label. The aftermath of the primary retained a bitter taste, as
few close to Valls became involved in the Hamon campaign and
the former premier committed the supreme act of treason by
announcing his vote for Macron before the first round.

In sum, the Republican (2016) and Socialist (2017) primaries destabilised party organisations, upset existing hierarchies and moved the putative presidential candidates to campaign in terms of core electors at the expense of the elusive median voter: witness Fillon's harsh attack on the French welfare state or Hamon's universal revenue. Combined with the partisan logic of the primary elections, the first-round logic of rallying core supporters was stronger than ever. Candidates gave primacy to first-round mobilisation over the anticipation of second-round strategies in 2017 because the outcome of the first round was far less certain than in any other recent presidential race (except arguably 2002). Macron was the exception. His successful positioning in terms of being anti-party and beyond left and right offered him a competitive advantage in the context where candidates of the traditional governing parties were above all turned inwards in the process of primaries. But were the primaries principally to blame for the collapse of the governmental parties? Did they really undermine the foundations of presidential institutions, weaken political parties and produce candidates who were unrepresentative of the broader electorate? Perhaps the primaries were not primarily at fault. As Grunberg and Haegel (2018) argue, the parties were deeply divided anyway; this is why the primaries took place in the first instance. The real crisis lay in the dangerously diminished legitimacy of political parties and their internal divisions.

Did the 2017 campaign make a difference to the outcome? There are three ways of answering this question, with varying degrees of sophistication. Fine-grained statistical analysis can be used to engage in electoral forecasting, a highly inexact science (Lewis-Beck, Nadeau and Bélanger, 2012). Other more qualitative work can accompany the campaign trajectories of individually selected voters (Gaxie, 2012). A third, blunter instrument can observe variation throughout the campaign in terms of the fortunes of the leading candidates. Of the various opinion poll instruments available, the most convincing was the CEVIPOF's 2017 election survey, a rolling survey of over 20,000 individuals that reported virtually on a monthly basis.[2] Table 4.1 presents the evolution of candidates' fortunes over the period of the eighteen months preceding the first round.

The first-round campaign was tightly fought, and there was genuine uncertainty about the outcome. The main dynamic in the run-up to 23 April appeared to be with Mélenchon, who excelled during the two televised debates, and Macron, who surfed on the anti-party wave as a candidate with a clean pair of hands, beyond left and right, who could be trusted to modernise France. Fillon and Le Pen both stagnated, while Hamon suffered from the Mélenchon dynamic and his own shortcomings. In 2017, Macron represented (for a while) the spirit of the times, as the repository of the electorate's general distrust in the mainstream parties and a candidate determined to clean up politics who could appeal to mainstream former Socialist and LR voters.

The extraordinary feature of the 2017 campaign, however, lay not so much in Macron's (relative) success as in the heavy underlying forces that swept aside the main parties in the presidential contest. First and foremost, there was the public's reaction against the 'scandals' involving the candidates, that of Fillon in particular, which prevented the electoral victory that most experts were predicting after the primaries. Second was the lack of focus on distributive, redistributive or regulatory political issues: the extraordinary climate of anti-politics produced a side-lining of the discussion of major issues of policy, a phenomenon that attracted interest and anxiety in foreign capitals. The deep unpopularity of President Hollande and the governing Socialists left little space for a defence of the 2012–17 mandate and the contradictory debate that this supposed. Moreover, even the European issue was blurred by the inconsistent positions adopted by Le Pen, Fillon, Hamon and Mélenchon. The FN's position on leaving the euro divided the movement itself and appeared to be called into question only days before the first round. Mélenchon struck a markedly anti-European tone, but refused to rule out remaining within the EU and the euro. Fillon and Hamon both struck a notably euro-critical note. Only Macron explicitly endorsed further European integration.

The campaign and results provided evidence of a deeply ingrained mistrust of the established political parties (in particular). Only one in four electors eventually voted for the candidates selected in the Socialist and Republican primaries. The crisis of the Socialists was particularly acute during the 2012–17 presidency; the first round sanctioned Hamon, one of the leaders of the *frondeurs*, whose comeuppance took the form of a humiliating 6.36%. For LR, Fillon's failure to win through to the second round (20.01%), after a campaign laid low by scandal, was not really a surprise.

Interpreting the 2017 electoral series

The danger of hyperbole was bound to be present following the qualification for the second round of Macron (24.01%) and Le Pen (21.3%). For the first time in the Fifth Republic, the candidate representing the mainstream Republican right (understood as comprising both the Gaullist and liberal-conservative traditions) did not win through to the second round; and while the Socialists failed in 1969 and 2002, the candidate they supported has also usually fought the run-off (in 1965, 1974, 1981, 1988, 1995, 2007 and 2012). Exit the two main governmental parties of the Fifth Republic. The situation was further blurred by the strong performance of Mélenchon (19.58%) and his unwillingness openly to support the 'globalist' Macron against the nationalist Le Pen.

Did the first round represent an earthquake? The metaphor is rather laboured. A volcanic outburst might be more accurate. But what type of volcanic eruption? A brutal Vesuvian eruption sweeping all aside in its wake? A Pompeii-style outburst, overwhelming, yet preserving remnants of the pre-existing order for the observance of posterity? A smouldering and spluttering Everest, ever threatening to erupt, but contained within its mountain range? There was evidence to support each of these positions, especially the first two.

The metaphor of a Vesuvian eruption implies a realigning election, in the sense of Pierre Martin (2000), in the French version of realignment theory. A realigning election represents first a moment of rupture, a radical break with the old order that takes the form of a paradigm shift; this is then followed by a realignment around new issues, in all probability channelled by new political organisations. The first round of the 2017 presidential election had the appearances of a radical break; the traditional governmental parties (PS and LR) obtained barely more than one-quarter of first-round votes (26.29% to be exact), down from well over one-half (55.81%) in 2012. On the other hand, the electoral verdict in 2017 was not totally unexpected. Recent presidential contests have taught us to expect the unexpected. In 2002, the announced second-round contenders (Chirac and Jospin) did not, in fact, win through to contest the run-off. In 2007, the third candidate Bayrou almost broke the mould; but his 18.57% was not quite enough to swing the election.

There is at least an argument that 2017 might represent a decisive break with the old order. The two second-round contenders were well positioned in terms of the two key defining features of the 2017 campaign: the rejection of existing parties and a clear position in terms of the cluster of progressive versus nationalist issues. While the rejection of the existing establishment parties was the defining feature of the electoral series, it is less clear that 2017 marked an ideological paradigm shift, as opposed to eclectic, random and inconsistent responses to the pressing policy issues of the day. Macron's programme was illustrative of this incremental approach: in line with the theme of co-construction, the programme itself was based on propositions tested in focus groups and on ideas received through its website and social media.

The fundamental ambiguities of Macron's campaign slogan *En même temps* ('At one and the same time') are developed in some detail in Chapter 5. One dimension of his central balancing act was his declared ambition to sweep aside the old party system of left and right, based on what were deemed outdated cleavages. The LRM candidate's most fertile territory was that of disillusioned former Socialist voters and politicians; the selection of a small number of PS deputies with the LRM ticket in the parliamentary elections following the presidential one gave a marker of centre-left intent, strengthened by the rallying of PS heavyweights such as Le Drian and Collomb. At the same time, and probably more consequentially, Macron's strategic agility led him to contest the territory of the centre-right. The nomination of the LR's Edouard Philippe, the mayor of Le Havre and a Juppé supporter, to the post of prime minister was a move designed to attract centre-right electors and divide the LR into Macron-compatible and unreconstructed elements. The creation of the parliamentary group known as the *Constructifs*, composed of deputies elected under the LR ticket in the 2017 parliamentary election but declaring themselves willing to support elements of Macron's policies on a case-by-case basis, was a vindication of Macron's strategy (the *Constructifs* were finally expelled from LR in October 2017, after months of internal wrangling). A similar pincer movement had already taken place with the PS.

'Out with the old' referred mainly to existing actors and parties. In terms of institutions, there was no rejection by Macron of the Fifth Republic nor a heeding of any bombastic call for a Sixth Republic (the project valued by Mélenchon and Hamon). The references made by Macron himself to the creation of the Fifth Republic in 1958 were highly indicative not only of his ambition, but also of a certain political style that was presented as being compatible with an early interpretation of the Fifth Republic. There was a reversion to one of the oldest traditions of the regime, in the form of the presidential rally. Macron's movement LRM bears some similarities with the UNR of 1958: it frames itself as both cross-party (picking the best talents) and anti-party (against the parties accused of undermining governmental authority and being self-serving); it places itself as being neither left nor right; it operates as a presidential rally to support an individual diagnosed as having exceptional qualities.

The 2017 campaign also produced symbolic positioning in terms of boundaries, borders and space. Marine Le Pen described the battle being fought as one between 'globalists' and 'patriots', while Macron identified a combat between 'progressives' and 'nationalists'. Macron positioned himself as the only unreserved pro-European, the one candidate calling for closer European integration as an instrument to assist economic modernisation and promote social justice. While rejecting the accusation of being 'naïve', moreover, Macron insisted that France could not simply ignore the reality of economic globalisation. Liberal in terms of social mores and respectful of plural French identities (hence more accommodating towards French citizens of immigrant origin), Macron also appeared as liberal in the economic sense in that he set out to reform labour law, encourage business innovation and investment and make France fitter for purpose in embracing the challenges of economic globalisation. Le Pen's programme was almost exactly the opposite: an 'intelligent' protectionism (taxation on imported goods), tough restrictions on immigration and a referendum on future membership of the euro.

These positions were reflected in the respective electoral support bases of the two candidates: Macron leading in the metropolises (Paris, Toulouse, Rennes, Lyon, Lille, Bordeaux and elsewhere); Le Pen ahead in *la France péripherique*, the lost small towns and rural areas between the larger cities (Guilluy, 2014). The centrality of the issue of cosmopolitanism versus nationalism cut across traditional lines of cleavage and blurred still further the boundaries between left and right. The positioning of Mélenchon was particularly significant in this respect: as a resolute opponent of Brussels and European integration. Mélenchon's reluctance to call explicitly upon his electors to support Macron on the second-round run-off was a further nail in the coffin of the Front Républicain (Republican Front, the alliance against the FN) and, indirectly, the traditional logic of left–right bipolarisation.

Macron's victory in the second round had been announced in advance (no opinion poll gave him less than 58% in the run-off), but it was more comfortable than initially imagined: 66.10% against 33.90% for Le Pen. The polls suggested that the margin of the final result was influenced by the second-round campaign and particularly by the candidates' televised debate, where an aggressive Marine Le Pen failed to destabilise Macron, lost her cool and, in contrast to her opponent, demonstrated little mastery of her policy dossiers. A survey credited Macron with having gained three percentage points as a direct result of the debate (ELABE, 2017). Macron won majorities in all *départements* save two (Pas-de-Calais and Aisne), while Le Pen had led in forty-seven (against forty-one for Macron) in the first round. The metropolises and sizeable cities overwhelmingly voted for Macron: 85% in Lyon, 83% in Marseille, almost 90% in Paris, 78% in Lille. The small towns and countryside voted for Le Pen – in places, at least. With 10,638,475 votes, Marine Le Pen obtained the best score ever for the FN, and more than doubled the total number of votes by comparison with her father in 2002. Macron polled twice as many (20,743,128), however, which put him well ahead of Sarkozy in 2007 and Hollande in 2012.

The aftermath: the parliamentary election

In the volcanic register, the second position – the Pompeii analogy – might be the most accurate. The existing world was overwhelmed in May 2017, but vestiges remained in the ruins, as became apparent in the June 2017 parliamentary election. Though seriously shaken and divided, the Republicans (LR) would live to fight another day, though it was unclear whether as much could be said for the PS. With Macron's election, the old world of left–right partisan politics appeared to be crumbling at the edges, but two key mechanisms of presidential power reaffirmed their pertinence: the confirmation election and the presidential party.

One of the core assumptions of the presidential-parliamentary electoral series is that the presidential election brings in its wake a comfortable majority for the victorious candidate in the subsequent parliamentary election. Since the 2000 constitutional reform and the inversion of the electoral calendar, there has been a powerful institutional incentive to provide the victorious president with the 'means to govern' by way of a large parliamentary majority. Of course, the presidential call for a parliamentary majority preceded 2000; most notable was that in 1981, when the victorious Socialist president François Mitterrand called on the people to 'give me the means to govern' and implement his presidential programme. But the relationship has become more mechanical since the 2000 reform changed the order of the electoral contests to ensure that the 'decisive' presidential election came before the 'confirmatory' parliamentary contest. Certainly, the figures have produced rather different variations of the presidential bonus since 2002, but on each occasion a party with a plurality of votes in the first round has achieved an absolute majority of seats after the second: the UMP in support of President Chirac in 2002, the UMP for Sarkozy in 2007 and the PS for Hollande in 2012. The 2017 parliamentary election confirmed the trend: with 32.55% of first-round votes, Macron's LRM obtained the overall parliamentary majority called for by the president, without needing the numerical support provided by its allies, Bayrou's Mouvement Démocratique (MODEM, Democratic Movement). The flip side was that this Herculean majority was based on a record low turnout for a parliamentary election in the Fifth Republic: 48.7% in the first round; 42.7% in the second. The confirmation election is implicitly based on a lesser popular mandate (and hence legitimacy) than the decisive presidential contest, though this distinction is nowhere formally recognised.

The victory of the LRM–MODEM ticket was announced so far in advance that its actual majority was considered to be somewhat disappointing – and certainly well below the true 'blue chambers' of 1993 and 2002.[3] The overall parliamentary victory was a remarkable achievement for a movement created barely one year earlier; it was crowned by the arrival in the National Assembly of a new generation of mainly inexperienced politicians, professionals and representatives of civil society (Ollion, 2017). The 2017 electoral series, however, left intact the overall crisis of confidence in the political system: not only was turnout in the two rounds of the parliamentary elections at an all-time low, but almost 10% cast a spoilt or invalid vote in the second round (see Table 4.2).

The first round of the parliamentary election confirmed the mechanical distrust and rejection of the incumbent parties: with 7.44%, the PS barely performed better than its presidential candidate, notwithstanding the advantage of incumbency. Even

Table 4.2 Votes and seats in the 2017 parliamentary election

Party	% (first round)	Seats (after second round)
Extreme left	0.77	0
PCF	2.72	10
LFI	11.03	17
PS	7.44	30
PRG	0.44	3
Other left	1.60	12
EELV	4.30	1
Other centre	2.21	3
Regionalists	0.90	5
LRM	28.21	308
MODEM	4.12	42
UDI	3.03	18
LR	15.77	112
Other right	2.76	6
Debout la France (France Upstanding)	1.17	1
FN	13.20	8
Extreme right	0.30	1
Abstentions (first round)	51.7%	
Spoilt and void ballots (first round)	1.08%	
Valid votes (first round)	47.62%	
TOTAL	100	577

Source: French Interior Ministry official figures, https://www.interieur.gouv.fr/Archives/Archives-elections/Elections-legislatives-2017/Premier-tour-des-elections-legislatives-resultats-globaux (last accessed 8 July 2018); https://www.interieur.gouv.fr/Archives/Archives-elections/Elections-legislatives-2017/Second-tour-des-elections-legislatives-les-resultats (last accessed 8 July 2018).

if we add EELV (4.30%),[4] PRG (0.44%) and other left parties (1.60%), the PS and its allies polled a bare 13% of those voting and were reduced to a rump parliamentary representation after the second round: the PS won 30 seats, PRG 3, other left parties 12, and EELV 1. The decline of the established parties was asymmetrical, however. LR and its allies performed marginally better (LR 15.77%, Union des Démocrates et Indépendants (UDI, Union of Democrats and Independents) 3.03%, other right parties 2.76%) and, above all, resisted better in the second round than its leaders had been expecting, returning a total of 135 deputies (LR 112, UDI 18, other right parties 6). Mélenchon's LFI elected 17 deputies, including Mélenchon himself in a Marseille constituency, but declined to 11.03% of first-round vote share. The PCF (2.72%) defended its bastions well, electing 10 deputies, and was able to form a parliamentary group with the support of a handful of overseas deputies. The FN (13.20%) was in steep decline from the first round of the presidential election and ended up with only eight deputies, including Marine Le Pen (one of five returned in the Pas-de-Calais *département*).

One of the routines of French parliamentary elections is for the smaller isolated parties to criticise the operation of the electoral system. To recall, France has a two-round system of voting in both presidential and parliamentary elections. In the latter contest, there are 577 single-member constituencies across the country. In order to be elected on the first round, an eligible candidate needs to obtain over 50% of valid votes and at least 12.5% of registered electors. In the event that a second round is necessary (and it usually is), only those candidates polling over 12.5% of registered electors go through to the second ballot. This 'majoritarian' electoral system usually gives an advantage in seats to the party with the most votes. 2017 was no exception. With 32.33% of first-round votes, the LRM–MODEM alliance obtained 350 deputies (rising to 359 once the parliamentary groups were formed) or 61% of the total, the second ballot system routinely inflating the number of seats obtained by the largest party. The second largest party – LR and allies – obtained 21.56% vote share, yet finished with almost 25% of seats. The main effect of the electoral system is to under-represent parties unable to form alliances: the case of the FN, with 13.20% of first-round votes yet under 2% of seats, is the most striking example.

The second mechanism was the return of the presidential party, or the majority elected primarily to support an incumbent president. True, the presidential party is a contested concept. And certainly, each presidential party has been different. De Gaulle's UNR had facets of a personal rally to a leader vested with a particular historic legitimacy, but it collapsed once the general had gone. Valéry Giscard d'Estaing's attempts to build the Républicains Indépendants (Independent Republicans) and Republican Party into the cornerstone of his UDF never really succeeded, and this failure undermined the cohesion of the 1974–81 mandate. On the left of French politics, many Socialists never really bought into Mitterrand's instrumental marriage of the incentive structure of the presidential institutions and the revival of party fortunes. Nonetheless, the election of a PS majority to back the president in 1981 provided a powerful political resource to ensure that Mitterrand got his way. The UMP (2002–12) reverted to form: the party of 'the right and the centre' was largely ignored by the successive presidents Chirac and Sarkozy, who saw its main function as being to organise the president's supporters in parliament. Macron's LRM can be seen as the latest version of the presidential party, and it is likely to follow a tested lifestyle: electoral triumph, the growth of internal dissensions, diminishing political returns and ultimate political defeat.

Whatever awaits, President Macron's coronation was now complete with the presidential majority that he had called for.

Notes

1   Marine Le Pen was accused of using European parliament funds to employ FN staff working in France. The case was ongoing at the time of writing.

2   There were eighteen waves, altogether, of the CEVIPOF–IPSOS– Sopra Steria *Enquête électorale française* published in *Le Monde*,

the authoritative rolling survey, which followed a panel of 21,326 registered electors through the ups and downs of the campaign from November 2015 to May 2018. All surveys are publicly available at https://www.enef.fr/ (last accessed 12 October 2018).

3   In 1993, the RPR–UDF had a large overall majority with 482 deputies out of 577. In 2002, the UMP and allies returned 398 out of 577 deputies.

4   A precautionary note: this total conflates those constituencies where EELV was allied to a PS candidate, as well as those where it stood alone or in alliance with LFI.

5

Macron's political leadership

ONE of the core enigmas of the 2017 presidential campaign related to the question: who is Emmanuel Macron? As the real prospect of his election drew nearer, the search for the 'real' Macron preoccupied journalists, commentators, political satirists and (rival) politicians, in more or less good faith. Did Macron represent the tardive manifestation in France of the Blairite Third Way, as suggested by Arnaud Parmentier (2017) in *Le Monde*? From a UK perspective, Macron seems so much like Tony Blair: young, handsome, charming, articulate, ruthless and driven to impose reforms. While there are some obvious similarities, Blair framed his leadership within one of the established parties, whereas Macron came from outside the existing party establishment. The specialist of the French right Gilles Richard sees Macron as a contemporary version of the liberal, Orleanist right, an adept of political and economic liberalisation (Richard, 2017). Rather more crudely, during the 2017 campaign Macron was painted as the representative of international finance by Marine Le Pen and Jean-Luc Mélenchon, in a not so strange convergence, while the LR candidate François Fillon portrayed him quite simply as the continuation of the (failed) Hollande presidency.

Even before his election as president, Macron was not a totally unknown quantity, of course. As deputy general secretary of the presidential staff from 2012 to 2014, he was a key figure in the background, exercising a reputedly strong influence in relation to the social liberal turn of the Hollande presidency (lowering taxes on business via the CICE business tax credit scheme of 2013 and the Responsibility Pact of 2014). As minister for the economy, industry and digital policy, Macron associated his name with a complex law that aimed comprehensively to modernise and liberalise the French economy; that most of its more controversial measures (especially in relation to the professions and work regulations) were abandoned or diluted was more a testament to the stout resistance of Socialist rebel deputies than evidence of half-hearted intent. In August 2016, Macron resigned from his position at the heart of the Hollande administration to undertake the risky venture of building his political movement (LRM, launched in April 2016) and standing for the French presidential election. At the very least, he is a political entrepreneur and a risk-taker.

Focusing on the individual qualities of a political leader is a necessary (though not sufficient) exercise (Burns, 1978). Most models of political leadership involve some combination of personal qualities or character traits, positional strengths and weaknesses, and wider environmental and cultural constraints and opportunities (Ahlquist and Levi, 2011; Berrington, 1974; Blondel, 1987; Drake, 2000; Edinger, 1990; Elgie, 1995; Foley, 2009; Gaffney, 2015; Helms, 1996). Understanding Macron requires a combination of three levels of analysis: the micro-level (individual qualities), the meso-level (institutional leadership) and the macro-level (Europe, foreign policy, the international economy). Political leadership results from the interplay between individual political style, institutional position and role and external constraints and opportunities. There is at least a heuristic value in combining levels of analysis if we are to understand Macron's activity as president.

Political persona

A stream of books and articles on Macron were published during and around the 2017 presidential election. These ranged from the hagiographical (Besson, 2017), through the psycho-biography (Fulda, 2016), to the philosophical (Couturier, 2017),or the instant or contemporary historical approach (Bourmaud, 2017a; Jeanneney, 2017; Prissette, 2017; Sirinelli, 2017) and the first attempts at conceptualisation and understanding Macron (Debray, 2017; Pedder, 2018). This first level of analysis is valuable, insofar as it disseminates representations that circulate and that are more or less tolerated and organised by the individual himself. Macron's personal qualities are understood and valued here insofar as they inform a broader political persona, which is defined by Marshall and Barbour (2015: 1) as 'a strategic identity, a form of negotiation of the individual in their foray into a collective world of the social'. Character traits are the heart of persona and play themselves out at three levels of abstraction: personal, symbolic and representative.

At the level of personal traits: the leadership qualities of decisiveness, strength, resolution, risk-taking, vision and imagination are differentially distributed, irrespective of wider structural circumstances. Not even his fiercest adversary can contest the ability to take risks; Macron's giving up his position as economy, industry and digital minister to launch himself into the risky venture of LRM demonstrated this. His resignation from the civil service so as to be able to contest the campaign went in the same direction. Some common themes that emerge in the above works are Macron's personal qualities of determination, resolution and brilliance, coupled with the image of the killer with a penchant for vertical forms of governing. The downside was the diffusion (in early surveys, at least) of the image of a rather arrogant, distant and elitist individual, a criticism that came to the fore during the Benalla scandal in July 2018.[1]

The category of personal attributes can be extended to those of immediate family. In the case of Macron, there is an argument that Brigitte, his spouse, played an important role in the overall political enterprise and that Brigitte and Emmanuel Macron formed a coherent political household, akin to that of the Pompidou family at an earlier period (Derrien and Nedelec, 2017). The foreign media in particular were obsessed with Brigitte Macron, who developed her own office within the Élysée, signed a transparency charter setting out her role and responsibilities and cultivated her image as a promoter of the liberal arts and various good causes. Macron learned from the mistakes of his two immediate predecessors in his handling of the 'peoplisation' of politics.[2] Rather than leaving personal life to chance, he deliberately and strategically shaped the narrative of his relationship with Brigitte, recruiting the head of the Bestimage agency, Mimi Marchand, in a successful effort to turn what (certainly in the Anglo-Saxon press) could have been the grubby backstory of a relationship between a man with a woman old enough to be his mother into a tale of triumphant romance that overturns ageist and sexist prejudices. The strategic use of Brigitte as part of a political household thus further enhanced Macron's personification of a generational change.

The personal dimension of Macron might also be understood at a second level of abstraction. His personal background is interesting insofar as he appears as a typical representative of the French elite, having studied at Sciences Po and the École Nationale d'Administration (ENA, National School of Administration). Rather like former President Pompidou, Macron also spent a period of time working in the private sector, for the Rothschild bank. In an IFOP poll published in the *Journal de Dimanche* of 16–17 March 2017, before his election, only 41% considered Macron to be close to the people (*Journal de Dimanche*, 2017); his background as a brilliant ENA graduate and his work for Rothschild bank leave the indelible impression that he is a member of the French elite. This representation is treated in a more nuanced way in some accounts. Abel (2017) insists on the fact that the young Macron studied for a higher degree in philosophy at Nanterre University and worked as editorial assistant for the philosopher Paul Ricœur, a reference that underpins the cultivated image of Macron as the president-philosopher, or, again, as the avid consumer of highbrow literature (Abel, 2017; Couturier, 2017; Mongin, 2017).

A rather different line of enquiry – still pertaining to character – relates to whether Macron embodies the spirit of the times, as the candidate who best crystallised the confused and contradictory ethos of a particular epoch. The focus here is not so much on individual qualities as on the symbolic function vested upon him. The strongest claim is that of generational renewal: he represented better than any other candidate the demand for a new generation. Elected president at thirty-nine years old, Macron was a few years younger than Tony Blair and around the same age as Matteo Renzi in Italy when they became premiers. Second, Macron's election symbolised the exhaustion of the traditional left–right cleavage in French politics: he was riding high on the rejection of party and contesting the validity of the left–right cleavage. For Taguieff (2017), Macron was both actor and subject of the withering-away of the old cleavage, and the embodiment of a new one, based on an openness–closure division within French society. For Baudry, Bigorne and Duhamel (2017), Macron is the symbol of the decomposition and recomposition of the French political system, a transformative position partially instigated by Macron himself. For Taguieff (2017), his success lies in the capacity to embody opposites: to be centrist and radical; to be courteous and ruthless; to appear as politically correct and anti-system. The key question is whether the equilibrist can put into effect a process of transformation. Valéry Giscard d'Estaing's old dream of representing two of every three French people ran into determined opposition and ultimately failed (Jeanneney, 2017). The Macron experiment deserves closer empirical observation, which will be the subject of the next section.

Macron's new institutional order

During the early days of his presidency, Emmanuel Macron positioned himself as the classical god Jupiter. Jupiter is above common mortals, and determines the fate of even the most powerful gods. This metaphor was intended to celebrate a return to authority and leadership at the heart of the State, a posture deliberately contrasted with the perceived failings of his three immediate predecessors: Chirac, Sarkozy and Hollande. The president cast himself as a quasi-divine Republican monarch, who symbolises the State and borrows the trappings of prestige from the pre-Revolutionary monarchy (as in his victory speech at the Louvre, and his reception of Russian President Vladimir Putin at the Versailles Palace, where he convoked the Congress a few weeks later) and whose rare parole gives meaning and direction to the nation. This construction was in obvious contrast with Hollande and his 'normal' presidency (Ignazi, 2018; Gaffney, 2015). Macron's positioning as Jupiter was intended not only to signify a return to sources of the Fifth Republic, but equally to impose an image, rather than allow a critical media to dictate a negative image, as in the case of Hollande and Flamby.[3]

Beneath the bombast and pretention, there is an argument that Macron understands the institutions of the Fifth Republic rather better than his predecessors, and certainly more than any other incumbent since Mitterrand (1981–95). Even before being elected president, he had declared himself to be an adept of 'vertical' relations at the summit of the State (Macron, 2016a). Underpinning this call lay the belief that the French wanted firm, purposeful leadership and that the Fifth Republic president came close to this desire for a monarchical-type figure. The Jupiter stance of the early months in office was carefully prepared, as was the strategy of making very rare public interventions (his first televised interview did not take place until October 2017). Such a position was increasingly difficult to maintain, however, as reforms gathered pace. And it was in direct conflict with another aspect of presidential strategy, namely 'telling the truth' and expressing preferences in the language of the people (hence Macron's use of provocative language designed to rally the people against established interests and the media and to support reform).[4]

In the Macron presidency, there is little room for doubt: the president determines the main orientations and sets out a road map for others (prime minister, government and parliament) to follow and implement. Macron is at the centre of interactions: the control over nominations concerned not only individual ministers (and the first amongst them, the prime minister) but also reached down into members of ministerial cabinets (Belouez-zane, 2017). In the words of one source cited by Perrineau (2018), 'Emmanuel Macron listens, but he always takes the main decisions alone.' The dangers of this method of governing lie in the risk of isolation, of being surrounded by courtesans and of losing contact with the country at large, a constant challenge faced by French presidents.

The presidential reach was demonstrated with the selection and composition of the Philippe governments in 2017. President Macron nominated the LR former mayor of Le Havre, Edouard Philippe, as prime minister at the head of a broad-based government comprising heavyweights from the PS (Jean-Yves Le Drian, Gérard Collomb), middleweights from LR (Gérard Darmintin and Bruno Le Maire) and various members of 'civil society' with impeccable professional credentials but who must be considered as lightweights in terms of their former political experience. In the composition of his governments (Philippe 1 and Philippe 2), former centre-right (LR) ministers were given the responsibility for economic affairs (Le Maire, Darminin), while experienced former PS ministers were given the core state functions of the interior (Collomb) and foreign policy (Le Drian). Prime Minister Philippe, close to Juppé, was drawn from the moderate and modernising wing of LR, a prize capture from the main right-wing party. Above all, however, the Philippe governments were dominated by specialist, non-party technicians in most fields of policy, such as education (Jean-Michel Blanquer), health (Agnès Buzin), social affairs (Muriel Pénicaud), culture (Françoise Nyssen) and environment (Nicolas Hulot, the former presenter of a popular television programme on the environment).

Macron's presidential reach went at least as far as that of previous presidents, and was symbolised by the practice of sharing presidential and prime ministerial advisors in key areas of public policy, of intervening in nominations in the semi-public economic sphere, of limiting the number of ministerial advisors and of involving top civil servants more publicly in the formulation and defence of government policy (Pietralunga, 2017). Those close to the inner circle refer to a tightly knit group of advisors labelled the Praetorian Guard or the Mormons. Macron surrounded himself with a brigade of young ambitious advisors at the Élysée, who formed a cordon sanitaire around the president and acted as the gatekeepers of presidential access (in marked contrast to his predecessor Hollande).[5] The general secretary of the Élysée staff, Alexis Kohler, was a fellow student at ENA; most other emblematic figures of the Macron regime had been students at Sciences Po Paris. As a former inspector of finances and economy minister, moreover, Macron has maintained a solid network at the Finance Ministry (Bercy), to the point of being accused in an anonymous tribune of higher civil servants published in *Le Monde* of allowing Bercy to dominate the policy formulation process (Collectif Léa Guessier, 2018; see also de Royer, 2017). The dangers of such a close commando-style of leadership became apparent during the Benalla scandal of July 2018, when footage was released of a presidential advisor beating up protesters at a 1 May demonstration (see note 1).

In terms of relations between president and prime minister, there is no room for diarchy, or two-headed leadership, at the top (though this has never really existed in the Fifth Republic, except perhaps with de Gaulle's premiers Debré and Pompidou). The order of protocol and priorities was clearly demonstrated in early July 2017, with President Macron addressing the two houses of parliament united in the Congress at Versailles on 3 July, followed by Prime Minister Philippe presenting the governmental programme to the National Assembly in Paris one day later (Fressoz, 2017). In his address to the Congress, on 3 July, Macron did not discuss details, but set out the contours of the transformation he intended to carry out. In his speech, on 4 July, Philippe presented the governmental programme in much more detail. All in all, this was a rather classical division of authority between the visionary president and the implementation of the presidential platform by the premier.

In his 3 July address to Congress, Macron announced his intention to reform the French constitution. At the heart of the constitutional reform proposals announced in July 2017, and formally published in April 2018, were a series of measures designed to rationalise French democracy in the name of efficiency: these included a reduction by one-third in the number of parliamentarians; the limitation for any one individual to holding three parliamentary mandates (as a deputy or senator) in a lifetime; the introduction of a measure of proportional representation in legislative elections; and the reform of the Economic and Social Council and the Higher Council of Magistrates. Whether these various measures would be approved as a constitutional amendment was far from certain at the time of writing. But they were highly illustrative of Macron's instrumental institutional vision, whereby the French parliament is perceived more in terms of a body for scrutiny and control of (presidentially determined) objectives than as a site for legislation and deliberation. Fewer deputies are likely to make fewer laws and spend their time in evaluation and scrutiny (the proposed constitutional amendment includes the provision to limit the ability of parliamentarians to propose amendments). The choice of the decree procedure (*ordonnances*) to implement emblematic policies (labour law, the reform of the national railway (the Société Nationale des Chemins de Fer, or SNCF) and professional training) was openly embraced as a means of speeding up procedure and minimising the delays of democratic deliberation. There is an argument that such rationalised parliamentary democracy is consistent with the spirit and practice of the Fifth Republic constitution (Camby, 2018). It remains the case, however, that this would be the first constitutional amendment to limit the powers of parliament, in contrast notably with the 2008 constitutional amendment enacted during Sarkozy's presidency.

The final instrument of presidential control is that of the party. Consistent with the Gaullist model of the very early Fifth Republic, LRM is a personal rally, where one individual makes all the real decisions (Magnaudeix, 2017). A strong central control has been exercised over the LRM parliamentary group. Very few deputies (*élus*) had a role to play during the presidential campaign. Once LRM was vested with an overall parliamentary majority, the dependency on Macron was even stronger, as these deputies had been elected to support the president. Macron has exercised close supervision over LRM, to the point of designating Christophe Castaner as its leader in November 2017 (Bourmaud, 2017b). LRM is purely the product of Macron. There are no party heavyweights, because they are not allowed to emerge (the territorial managers known as 'referents' are named by the central party, and there are no presidents of party federations, as in the PS, for example). There is little contact with the media, and there are few convincing LRM voices in the public debate (as opposed to ministers in Philippe's government). Very few LRM deputies had prior national-level party political experience; only twenty-seven (of 309) were previously deputies, nearly all of them from the PS. LRM deputies openly envisaged their roles as becoming technical experts in particular domains, as part of a broader managerial culture. As a result of its origins as a political start-up, LRM has been marked by the search for new ideas and policies rather than structures, and a relative disinterest in training party cadres. And yet it has now to face up to the challenges of organising support for the president and laying down the roots of a genuine party organisation to fight the 2019 European and – especially – 2020 municipal elections.

From the UK's perspective, LRM is remarkable precisely because it appeared to emerge from nowhere, a political start-up led by a ruthless entrepreneur. The success of LRM certainly tells us something about the state of decay of the other parties, and especially the PS, discussed in Chapter 3. In comparison with the UK, it would appear to be relatively straightforward to start up a new party in France; it has proved impossible for a new centre party to get off ground level in the UK, and parties such as the Social Democratic Party, the Referendum Party and even the United Kingdom Independence Party (UKIP) were failures. The success of 'Macron and Company' focuses attention on the extreme personalisation of party competition that is encouraged by the French presidential election and was pushed to its extreme in 2017 as a result of the discredit of the main Republican formations, the PS and LR. Not only Macron, but also Le Pen and Mélenchon were political beneficiaries of this ground movement.

It remains to be seen whether such movements are sustainable in the long run.

The master of time

The positioning of Macron as the Greek god Jupiter was intended to give a new sense of purpose to political choices in the register of transformative political leadership. It would be an act of bad faith to accuse Macron of not putting his campaign promises into operation. The Macron presidency has, thus far, revealed itself to be one of the most ambitious and reformist in the history of the Fifth Republic. Around a dozen major fields were opened in the first few months, with clear sequences intended to give meaning to political action throughout the five-year period (Robin, 2017). After a shaky start – the sacking of the chief of staff of the army, the poor reception of cuts (specifically to housing benefits) announced across governmental budgets without prior negotiation, the obvious inexperience of several new ministers and members of the governing LRM party – the early months of the presidency followed, fairly clearly, the road map announced by the president. The speed and rhythm of the reform programme cast Macron as a new 'fast president', announcing multiple reforms in a blitzkrieg designed to destabilise the opposition and rather reminiscent of the early period of Sarkozy (2007–08) or of Blair (1997–98). The 2017–18 reform programme was an ambitious one, and most sectors were represented: the moralisation of politics, the reform of labour law, a new internal security law, the abolition of the wealth tax, the changing rules for university entrance, the reform of the unemployment insurance and training regimes, immigration reform, prison reform, civil service reform, the overhaul of school examinations (the Baccalaureate) and even the sacred cow of the special statute for national railway workers. Two early laws were particularly symbolic: the law on the moralisation of French politics forbade the practice of employing family members as staff members and placed limits on expense claims; the decrees reforming the labour code (enhancing firm-level bargaining, limiting severance pay, reforming the operation of trade unions, especially in the smallest firms, simplifying and unifying staff representative committees in the workplace) were intended to modernise France's system of industrial relations and encourage investment.

In the case of Macron, as with Sarkozy a decade earlier, a clear presidential mandate was followed by a vigorous programme of social and economic reforms. In both cases, also, an active presidential leadership was framed as the antithesis of an earlier period of stasis; the immobile Chirac for Sarkozy, or the compromised Hollande for Macron. In both cases, the speed of reforms was designed to destabilise adversaries and exploit to the maximum the window of opportunity opened by precise circumstances. Both used practices from the Anglo-Saxon world of triangulation (adopting adversaries' policies as a destabilising tool). In the case of Macron, finally, there is an explicit use of nudge theory, whereby citizens are provided with clear incentives to make the right choices.

The strategic management of time formed a key part of Macron's planned approach. During the first year, reforms were closely sequenced, being designed to underline that the president alone is the 'timekeeper' (*le maître de l'horloge*). The first six months were intended to represent an economic sequence designed to set France on a course of economic reform and competitiveness; the next period – rather less convincingly – was intended to re-balance, to offer a social counterpart to economic reform. The strategic dimension of time management could be illustrated with the 2018 budget. The headlines of the 2018 budget concerned the powerful symbolic abolition of the wealth tax, along with the adoption of a 30% 'flat tax' to encourage investment in the 'real' economy and risk-taking. The main novelty, however, was to move towards a five-year budgetary logic. The announcement of spending priorities and commitments across the five-year period (2018–22) was intended to modify the meaning of the annual budget cycle, with a view to ensuring fiscal and policy stability over the medium term and encouraging investment. In the case of Macron, an overarching strategic time frame (the budget, the five-year presidential term as a whole) is coupled with a clever tactical use of time: involving social partners in consultation, floating ideas subsequently to be watered down and forcing deadlines on negotiations. There was a clear method. The announced reforms followed a similar pattern: the promise of consultation (but not negotiation) with social partners and other interested parties; a strictly controlled government timetable; the announcement of ambitious targets to be achieved; a stated preference for the procedure of decrees and limited parliamentary oversight; and a strong investment in new instruments of central steering (for example the creation of a territorial agency for local government and a new training agency).

En même temps: the elusive equilibrium

The Macron enterprise has been built on the rejection of the main party families and the mantra of *en même temps*. *En même temps* can be read first as a campaign slogan – rather like Obama's 'Yes we can'. The literal translation – 'on the one hand, on the other hand' – might be subject to confusion, however. It can imply an equilibrist, between left and right, the traditional positioning of the centre in France. Identifying itself as between left and right, the French centre has traditionally been squeezed between the Scylla of anti-Gaullism and the Charybdis of anti-Socialism, with a tendency for the centre to drift towards the latter position. The rallying of the historic centrist Bayrou in February 2017 put Macron's flagging campaign back on track; the debt to the traditional centre was acknowledged by the freshly elected Macron, who rewarded Bayrou with a major position in government and ensured that the MODEM was generously endowed with winnable seats in the June 2017 parliamentary elections (at which it elected forty-two deputies). But renewing with a certain legacy of the French centre is only a small part of the Macron story. *En même temps* can also imply a transformative leader beyond left and right, consigning the key ideological cleavage drawn from the

French Revolution to history; the 'old' system condemned by Macron and supporters is roundly rejected, in terms of both the mutually exclusive ideological frames it embodies and the parties it produces which feed on maintaining ideological exclusivities for instrumental partisan advantage (Darrigand, 2017). Third, *en même temps* can be understood as both left and right. In this third synthesis, left and right provide inspiration, ideas and talented people on which a modernising president should draw. The historical precursors are General de Gaulle in 1945 and 1958, Prime Minister Rocard in 1988 and even President Sarkozy in 2007: on each occasion, political leaders attempted to draw in the best talents from across the political spectrum. The political leader is likened to the curator of a museum, classifying the contributions made by left and right and drawing in the best talents, ideas and political programmes, whatever their provenance. These three positions – centre, central, custodial – are not identical, however, and imply a permanent process of adjustment (between social protection and economic liberalisation, for example). They can also produce confusion and ambiguity. Macron's own strategists admitted to the difficulty of defining Macronism as a core political project (Lemarié and Pietralunga, 2018).

En même temps assumes some sort of balance between the social and economic dimensions of freedom and protection. As the Macron presidency progressed, this balance appeared to be called into question. Opinion surveys began to register a sense of injustice after several months of frenetic, but rather inconsistent, reforms mainly centred on economic modernisation: hence an ELABE survey of March 2018 indicated that 74% considered Macron's reforms to be socially unjust (ELABE, 2018). The image of the 'president of the rich' stuck to Macron, as he abolished the wealth tax in his first budget; former President Hollande stirred up existing enmities by describing his successor as the 'president of the very rich' (Morin, 2018). The polls began to tell a consistent story, whereby Macron was much more popular amongst centre-right electors than amongst those situating themselves on the centre-left. While Macron had a clear message in terms of economic reform, he was less audible in terms of social policy, on societal issues related to French identity and multiculturalism, or in relation to how to deal with peripheral France (*la France péripherique*), that fragile space identified by geographers in rural and small-town areas. The violent criticism of Macron's metropolitan-centric focus levelled by the LR leader Laurent Wauquiez made some impact, as did his criticism of narrow Paris-based elites. The symbol of Macron's supposed imperviousness to the demands of rural populations lay in the reduction of the speed limit from 90 km to 80 km per hour on secondary roads. This was deeply unpopular, with 71% opposed to reducing the speed limit according to a You Gov survey of May 2018 (Botella, 2018), though, paradoxically, it was steered by Prime Minister Philippe, rather than Macron himself.

En même temps also presupposes some sort of balance between left and right. One of the claims of Macron's support-ers was to have exploded the old system of parties and the underlying left–right cleavage. And all parties that ride on the left–right cleavage are in a sorry state. But the rise of tensions within LRM itself revealed that left and right remained emotive categories on questions of identity and values. In an interview with the author, one of the remaining PS deputies claimed he had met 'left en marche and right en marche, but never pure en marche'. This ideological eclecticism was illustrated by the reaction to the interior minister Collomb's December 2017 circular in relation to migrants, which called upon prefects to monitor the presence of illegal immigrants in emergency housing centres, creating divisions even within LRM. These divisions were bought to the fore by bitter LRM divisions over the immigration and asylum law, approved by the National Assembly in May 2018. A reaction to this hard line on migration lay behind the first attempt to structure a left-wing tendency within LRM. After one year of office, the support for Macron amongst intellectuals and professionals was beginning to wither: for example, Jean-Paul Pisani, Macron's key economist during the campaign, Laurent Berger of the Confédération Française Démocratique du Travail

(French Democratic Labour Federation) and the Nobel prizewinner Jean-Marie Le Clezio were all critical of the lack of a more ambitious social agenda.

The Macron narrative had to accommodate other internal contradictions. One such tension is that between transparency and confidentiality. Macron used the language of the blocked society to justify his call for thoroughgoing change during the campaign. Introducing more transparent, open forms of government was the leitmotif of his campaign message. The linguistic component of this claimed transparency is one of telling the truth, 'saying' as a prelude and accompaniment to 'doing'. In his first television interview since being elected (15 October 2017), Macron repeated pointedly 'I do what I say' (TFI, 2018), a stance that recalled the 'telling the truth' mantra of the former premier Michel Rocard (1932–2016). A favourable presidential image based on telling the truth was diffused in the main successfully during the first year in office. If there appeared to be diminishing returns after the first year, this was in part because of the natural leadership cycle, but also because the gap between the coherence of presidential action and discourse became more marked during the second year in office. Mixed messages and doubtful metaphors blurred the clarity of the early message – even more than the lack of concrete policy results.

Implicit in the stance of telling the truth is the promise of a clear legitimising discourse around change (why it is necessary and what it implies), as well as a pedagogical commitment to justify the need for change or at least to convince doubters of the well-founded and necessary nature of reforms. Once Macron had been elected president, however, secrecy formed a part of his mode of governance (Bonnefous, Pietralunga and de Royer, 2017). Determined to avoid the multiple *couacs* (literally, false notes) of the Hollande administration, Macron insisted on signing confidentiality clauses with members of the government, with the result that there have been very few governmental leaks and the media have been held at a distance. The processes within the LRM party were also guided by principles of confidentiality and hierarchy (Lemarié and Rescan, 2017). The negative effects of the Benalla affair of July 2018 highlighted the dangers of this secretive leadership style and practice: namely, that presidential advisors could exercise undue influence and that Macron did not deign to respond to public or media criticism.

Another inconsistency within Macron's narrative lies in the interplay between authority and democracy. Macron's presidential programme, published in early March 2017, was justified by the candidate in terms of actively mobilising citizens in its co-construction. The campaign laid stress on mobilising the energies of the people to transform society. Metaphors of the start-up nation were encouraged by the candidate himself to encourage the image of EM (both Emmanuel Macron and his campaign slogan *En marche!*) as a political start-up based on the mobilisation of civil society – and this non-political dimension was fully represented in Philippe's government. But, as Perrineau (2018) points out: 'once in power, Macron's belief in civil society gave way to a concentration on experts and expertise'. The great reform wave of 2017–18 demonstrated a preference for management solutions, for rule by experts and professionals rather than career politicians, for a focus on policy outcomes and results (what works and how can it be measured) rather than for exploring new forms of democratic participation.

Finally, *en même temps* appeared to be of limited efficacy in responding to unforeseen crises and sudden shifts in the issue agenda. The issue of migration exemplifies this well. Migration was barely raised as an issue at all during the 2017 campaign – by Macron, at least. Insofar as he articulated a position, Macron's attitude appeared to be at odds with the firm stance expressed by the former premier Valls, who was critical of German 'laxism' and the admission of hundreds of thousands of migrants in 2015. But migration is one of those issues where neatly balanced positions are difficult to achieve. Macron's response to the migrant crisis was one of apparent inconsistency. In early June 2018 President Macron harshly criticised the new Italian interior minister Salvini for refusing to allow the *Aquarius*, a vessel carrying rescued migrants, to dock in Italy; in late June 2018, he publicly condemned the NGO Lifeline for rescuing another group of migrants. In this case, Macron proved to be an irritant to both sides in the debate. This stance, repeated in other policy fields, appeared to be inconsistent, if not improvised, a sentiment captured by polls after the first year in office.

Just how well rooted and sustainable is *en même temps*, however, when it is built mainly on a rejection of the old party families and system? Experts such as Marc Lazar (2018a) confess to a persistent difficulty of positioning 'Macronism' in the long term as a phenomenon between left and right, while Jeanneney (2017) is of the opinion that left and right will re-emerge in some form or another, and Juillard (2018) points to the robust health of social democracy and conservatism as central references in French political culture. Macron's movement LRM, as its title suggests, is focused more on movement and action than on vigorous philosophical consistency. In sum, *en même temps* proved to be a good campaign slogan, but rather lightweight as a principle for managing public affairs.

On the first anniversary of his election as President of the French Republic, Emmanuel Macron could make a credible claim to have imposed a new style and rhythm on French politics, characterised by a vertical chain of command; a distrust of intermediaries (parties, trade unions, interests) between the president and the people; a robust form of political expression, based on an explicit rejection of left and right and organised political parties; and a routine dismissal of the 'old world'. The enterprise encountered a measure of domestic success, if we are to believe Macron's poll ratings after one year in office (he was more popular in various surveys at this stage than Sarkozy or Hollande). The drive to reform France domestically during the first year was, in part, a function of restoring the country's good name on the European and global level, the theme that is addressed in the next chapter.

Notes

1   The scandal broke in mid-July 2018, when videos of Alexandre Benalla, one of President Macron's key security advisors, were published by *Le Monde*, allegedly showing Benalla roughing up

a couple of protestors during the 1 May 2018 demonstrations in Paris. The scandal involved, *inter alia*, the interior minister (Gérard Collomb), the chief of the Paris police force (Michel Delpuech), the head of Macron's own office (Patrick Stzroda) and, some would argue, Macron himself. It cast light on the malfunctioning of the security services under Macron and the willingness of his advisors to take the law into their own hands. The scandal was interpreted in the press as highly informative of Macron's leadership style, which is based on the primacy of a network of personal loyalties, developed in the main during the 2017 presidential campaign, to the exclusion of professional and political influences from outside the inner circle.

2   I am grateful to one of the anonymous readers for this point.

3   Flamby was a nickname invented by opponents to describe François Hollande as soft and inconsistent. The allusion to a popular dessert did great damage.

4   In a register close to that of former President Sarkozy, Macron has taken to speaking the language of the people, criticising the lazy ('les faineants') who don't want to work; professing 'I'm not Father Christmas' when faced with demands for Guyanese demonstrators for the massive aid and development package promised by the previous government; lamenting the 'unreformable character' of the French; denigrating those 'people who are nothing' who took to demonstrating against his government's reforms; and condemning the 'lazy' and the 'illiterate'.

5   For example, Ismaël Emelien was reputedly a very influential presidential advisor and a key gatekeeper of access to the president.

6

Global Macron

EUROPEAN and foreign affairs are sometimes presented as the traditional 'reserved domains' of the French president, where decisions are reserved for the president (Irondelle, Joana and Mérand, 2016). The idea of a reserved domain is not literally true, of course, as there are many other actors involved in the European and international security policy communities, from the armed and security forces, through leaders in other countries, to actors in international organisations and think tanks. The formal machinery of government itself represents a powerful foreign policy bureaucracy. The French Foreign Affairs Ministry comprises a vast, extensive network of career diplomats and diplomatic representations, second only to that of the US in global coverage. The foreign affairs and defence ministers are actively involved in foreign policy, as is the prime minister (for example Edouard Philippe under Macron). But the French president incarnates French foreign policy grandeur more than any of his European counterparts or other potential domestic rivals, a point repeatedly made in presidential memoirs (most recently, Hollande, 2018). Nowhere is the Gaullist framing of the French president's role as incarnating 'greatness' more relevant than in the sphere of foreign policy, and it is lent credibility on account of France's status as the leading continental military power with its own independent nuclear force. In a rather similar way, France has always considered herself to occupy a leading role in European affairs; if presidential incarnation is somewhat less marked or convincing, France is a leading member-state and the French president a key European player.

The title of this chapter – 'Global Macron' – describes a politician who has fully integrated the global dimension of politics into the construction of his domestic political leadership (Frachon, 2017). Two decades earlier, the UK premier Tony Blair was being described and analysed in similar terms (Smith, 2007). By the time of the Davos summit in February 2018, Macron felt sufficiently confident to declare that 'France is back'. His claim to have restored the rank of France is made first of all in relation to Europe.

Macron's European window of opportunity: double or bust?

From the outset, there has been an explicit linkage between domestic and European politics. But are domestic styles and remedies transferable to the European scene? The first year of Macron's presidency was rather inconclusive in this respect.

That Macron has made an impact is not open to doubt. In recognition of his contribution to the ideal of European union, he was awarded the prestigious Charlemagne Prize in May 2018, becoming the first French president to have been thus honoured, since in 1988 the then President Mitterrand and Chancellor Helmut Kohl were joint recipients of the award. The Charlemagne Prize was awarded mainly in recognition of the 2017 campaign itself, where Macron had been the only candidate explicitly endorsing enhanced European integration. Through his election in May 2017, Macron was widely credited with stemming the rise of populism after the Brexit referendum, at a critical juncture in European history – shortly before Germany, Austria and Italy would each in their own way call into question the reality of a new European consensus. Be that as it may, Macron's activism in favour of a new European deal contrasted very starkly with the inaction of his predecessors Chirac (after the 2005 referendum defeat), Sarkozy and Hollande. Macron's European vision was articulated in four key speeches: at the Acropolis in Athens in August 2017, at the Sorbonne University, Paris, in September 2017, at the European parliament in Strasbourg and at Aachen in May 2018.

As in domestic politics, once elected President Macron enjoyed a seemingly favourable set of circumstances in Europe. Quite apart from the moral credit of being elected as the only explicitly pro-European candidate in the French presidential election, Macron's capacity to articulate a European vision contrasted with that of France's main neighbours and partners. The self-exile of the UK via the Brexit process presents challenges and opportunities for France, but in the short run it removed a competitor, notably in the field of European security and defence policy. Macron's dynamic leadership contrasted with the decline of that of Chancellor Merkel, with the federal elections of September 2017 being followed by five months of coalition bargaining before a chastened alliance of the Christlich Demokratische Union (CDU, Christian Democratic Union) and Christlich-Soziale Union (CSU, Christian Socialist Union) finally agreed to renew its coalition agreement with the Sozialdemokratische Partei Deutschlands (SPD, Social Democratic Party of Germany). In some respects, the withering of Angela Merkel, after over a decade of uncontested European leadership, presented challenges for Macron, but it also allowed the French president to reclaim a certain leadership role in Europe. The traditional Mediterranean countries that looked to France for leadership, or at least alliance – Spain and Italy – were both in a state of stasis. The Spanish premier Rajoy was confronted with the Catalan crisis in Spain and was eventually forced to resign after a vote of no confidence in the Spanish parliament, being replaced by Pedro Sanchez at the head of a minority government. In Italy, the inconclusive election of March 2018 – marked by the rise of the League and the Five Star Movement – eventually produced a fragile government led by Giuseppe Conti, but driven by the League's Matteo Salvini. Both Spain and Italy were ill-placed to launch European initiatives. At the same time, the hardening of relations with several of the countries of central and Eastern Europe – though dangerous in some respects – provided Macron with an opportunity to deliver on one of his domestic commitments (the reform of the posted workers' directive). In this confused European context, Macron diagnosed a window of opportunity for European reform in a manner consistent with French preferences.

His European vision was central to his speech at the Sorbonne (26 September 2017), renewing in an act somewhat reminiscent of Mitterrand in the 1980s and early 1990s. In his Sorbonne speech, the French president called for a European relaunch, characterised by a more integrated foreign, security and defence policy; more EU-wide defence procurement; measures to tackle the democratic deficit at the EU level (reforms of the European parliament, the introduction of EU-wide constituencies for the European elections, a new democratic dialogue across Europe); procedures for differentiated integration, where groups of member-states could engage in 'enhanced cooperation' in specific areas; and a Europe that 'protects' its citizens (reforms of the posted workers' directive) and its industries (from Chinese assault, notably). The most ambitious EU proposals related to the governance of the euro-zone. Macron argued in favour of the creation of a euro-zone super-minister, with a separate dedicated budget, and the transformation of the European Security Mechanism into a fully pledged European Monetary Fund, all to be supervised by a new euro-zone parliament. These positions were a powerful restatement of French preferences: namely, to ensure political supervision of the governing mechanisms for the euro (the super-minister), to facilitate transfers from richer countries (especially Germany) to poorer ones in the name of economic convergence and solidarity, and to endow the EU with new fiscal resources. Macron's European *en même temps* reconciled a staunch belief in the merits of European integration with a recognition that it was essential to renew the citizenship compact after a tough decade of economic reform. The substance of the new European grand bargain reflected French preferences in other fields also. His call for there to be a Europe-wide consultative process – the EU conventions, modelled on his own practice (*les marcheurs*) – was given a polite reception in Brussels and in most European countries.

Ultimately, the limits of the Macron enterprise lay in the need to build the necessary coalitions (first and foremost with Merkel) and to demonstrate the economic success of the French model. In a rather predictable construction, Macron looked to the Franco-German relationship to assume a central role; the terms of this tied the success of the window of opportunity to developments in Germany, France's main political partner, though figures published in 2018 had seen France retroceding to the fourth place in terms of economic exchanges with Germany. For months, the Macron proposals were met with a constrained, polite silence from Germany. After the German elections of September 2017, the CDU–CSU–SPD coalition agreement which eventually emerged (in March 2018) was potentially more favourable to Macron's grand bargain than the alternative failed Jamaica coalition (the CDU, CSU, Frei Demokratische Partei (FPD, Free Democratic Party) and Greens).

The reception of the Macron agenda in Brussels and other EU capitals was mixed. The CDU–SPD coalition agreement, published in March 2018, did not mention the euro-zone minister (Hughes, 2018). It soon became apparent that the temperature in the new Merkel-led coalition was lukewarm to the French proposals, with the Germans traditionally reluctant to entertain ideas of the mutualisation of euro-debts or to agreeing to more fiscal transfers within the euro-zone. In the context of the rise of Alternative für Deutschland (Alternative for Germany) in 2017, the Germans have other priorities: ensuring more pan-European solidarity in relation to migration and refugees in particular. Moreover, the new German coalition was divided on issues of European solidarity and a more integrated EU defence policy, matters of great concern to French President Macron. Macron's call for there to be EU-wide lists for elections to the European parliament was specifically rejected by the European parliament. His proposal for creating a euro-zone parliament, which echoed that of his predecessor Hollande, faced hostility from Berlin as well as from the European Commission, for whom the European parliament already provides a democratic oversight of EU institutions. And his call for a separate budgetary chapter for the euro-zone economies – if understandably well received amongst the euro-zone 'sinners' in southern Europe – provoked eight northern EU states led by the Netherlands to publish their own rebuttal of the road map and to restate the importance of respecting the rules of euro membership.

Does this episode demonstrate the victory of style over substance? Such a judgement would be a harsh one. At the very least Macron has restored France's seat at the table; there has been a credible restatement of the Franco-German relationship and its role in driving major new policy initiatives (the 'road map' agreed by Macron and Merkel in March 2018 and presented to the EU summit of June 2018). Nonetheless, the European Commission's draft budgetary perspectives for 2021–27 represented a direct challenge to traditional French priorities in agriculture by advocating cuts to the Common Agricultural Policy. The proposed creation of a modest budgetary line for the euro-zone would appear to fall well short of Macron's proposals for a very substantial budget to oversee transfers to the poorer euro-zone members as a measure of solidarity. There are obvious questions to be asked in relation to the goodness of fit between domestic and European leadership styles. There is arguably no office more capable of expressing an idealistic European vision than that of the French presidency, especially as personified by Emmanuel Macron. It remains to be seen how the French president's holistic European vision will fare when confronted with the realities of EU bargaining and the continuing attraction of alternative narratives of the future of Europe.

Global Macron

A global presence is one of the classic roles of French presidents, the role model having been defined almost seven decades ago by General de Gaulle. The image of the French president as a supra-partisan Republican monarch depends in part on fulfilling the noble functions of the State: representing the unity of the nation abroad and symbolising national unity during times of war and peace. French presidents have traditionally claimed a 'reserved domain' in foreign policy and defence – and very clearly Macron is no exception. Key foreign and defence policy decisions and initiatives taken are taken at the Élysée, either by Macron or in his regular meetings with the chiefs of staff (Guisnel, 2018). Macron assumes the normal function of a French president: the prominent role in European affairs and in defence and security policy, as well as the personalisation of relations with foreign leaders such as Donald Trump. The phrase 'Global Macron' also refers to a very personalised foreign policy leadership, involving a downscaling of the foreign affairs minister, Le Drian, who had occupied a much more prominent role as defence minister under Hollande's presidency.

From the outset, Macron measured himself against the great and the good in world politics. Within two months of his election, he had welcomed the Russian leader Vladimir Putin with great pomp and ceremony to the Versailles Palace and US President Trump to the 14 July display of military hardware on the Champs-Élysees. During his first year, Macron led formal state visits to China, Algeria, India and the US, *inter alia*, which combined diplomacy with trade and cultural promotion. Substantively, also, under Macron, the French president was seen once again to be performing an active role in terms of foreign policy. Amongst the many examples, let us mention the attempts to reaffirm the centrality of an eventual French role as mediator in the Middle East and to mediate the Lebanon–Saudi Arabia crisis in late 2017.

There are important differences in relation to his immediate predecessors. From the very beginning of his mandate, Macron has been more than a traditional French foreign policy president; he is representative of a Macron brand, admired elsewhere, a model of youthful, reformist and intentional political leadership. He symbolises renewal on the international scene, as well as domestically, the French president being the most prominent of a new generation of world leaders also including Canada's Justin

Trudeau. The generational effect has spilled over from domestic to foreign policy, inspiring the young president to enter into a world dialogue with other young people (witness the importance placed on addressing student audiences in Bamako or Washington, as well as in Paris, reinforcing the subliminal message that a new generation is now in command). Finally, Macron also stands apart from his predecessors insofar as celebrity politics has spilled over into the international sphere, with Brigitte Macron a key part of the presidential toolkit. If political leadership is in part a form of communication, Macron is a past master, an adept of personal stage management, including a much more prominent use of Brigitte Macron and 'private' visits such as that to the Taj Mahal in India in 2018 (de Royer, 2018). In international affairs also, the close collaboration with popular magazines such as *Paris Match* or *Vanity Fair* is in stark contrast with the distant relationships maintained with more critical media outlets (the quality press and the twenty-four-hour news programmes in particular).

Macron has challenged elements of the traditional repertoire. French presidents usually deliberately assume a position of national unity abroad; such was the case for President Hollande, for example, in Mali or Syria. The logic of national consensus usually encourages political leaders to rise above domestic conflict. Not so Macron, who has used distance from home to publicly reiterate the theme of the difficulty of reforming French society, to announce (to the rest of the world) his determination to continue to reform. Herein lies another aspect of the Janus-faced nature of the Macron presidency. It involves a permanent two-way dialogue, playing up domestic reforms in order to strengthen national prestige abroad while using the foreign arena to reinforce the reform message at home, in a permanent movement and transition between levels. Foreign leaders and audiences are invited to be fellow conspirators in the plot to reform and change French society. Global Macron represents a permanent interaction between personality, position and environment.

There are limits to this enterprise. In practical terms, the frequent absences from France (forty-six days abroad during the first six months of 2018) produced growing criticism at home. For a system that relies so heavily on personal direction, Macron's physical absence created a vacuum (witness the spat between the finance minister Bruno Le Maire and his associate Gérard Darminin in relation to welfare spending, or Prime Minister Edouard Philippe's inability to formulate clear policy responses without the physical presence of the president). In terms of substance, too, the *en même temps* doctrine is less easy to export to the global – or even European – stage. The French president seeks to articulate a somewhat contradictory international message, one that is less easy to justify in terms of the domestic register of *en même temps*. It is caught between the need to promote France as a mover of international free trade and liberalisation – the 'France is back' of the 2018 Davos summit – and the domestic agenda of a France that protects against globalisation. What passes for creative compromise at home represents a blurring of the message internationally. The positive framing of such a position is that France 'speaks with everyone' and is respected as an interlocutor. Under Macron, France has indeed attempted to be more present in the Middle East, in Africa and in Asia. But the balanced stance probably overplays French capacity: visits to Iran and Russia by the foreign affairs minister Le Drian, for example, made no difference to the activities of Iran and Russia in Syria. And Macron had little influence over the Turkish leader Recep Erdoğan or the Israeli prime minister Benjamin Netanyahu. The *en même temps* doctrine also appeared to be inconsistently applied when he was faced with authoritarian political leaders, depending on French interests. There was a clear inequality of treatment between Egypt's General Sisi – a harsh authoritarian leader who had purchased French Rafale planes – and the Turkish leader Erdoğan.

And then there is the specific case of US President Trump, where Macron arguably overplayed his hand and discovered the perils of investing too much faith in a 'special' personal relationship. All started so well. President Trump's state visit to France in July 2017 was heavy in state symbolism, the US president declaring himself to be impressed by the 14 July display of military hardware on the Champs-Élysées. French participation in the US-led air strikes in Syria, alongside the UK, confirmed France's status as a key US ally. The pomp and glory of Macron's visit to the US in in May 2018 contrasted with the frosty reception received by Chancellor Merkel later in the same week. And yet this was all to little effect, as Trump successively withdrew the US from Paris climate agreement and then from the Iran nuclear agreement, before finally imposing trade tariffs on steel and aluminium and sparking fears of a global trade war. Macron's *en meme temps* was not designed to confront such realist power plays.

In conclusion, Macron's political leadership appeared as a successful political construction after his first year in office. In the expression of Marshall and Barbour (2015: 1), persona 'helps the individual navigate their presence and interactions with others and helps the collective to position the role of the individual in the social'. Macron's political leadership is best understood in terms of a permanent interaction and negotiation between persona (individual characteristics in a social setting), position (institutional context) and environment (mainly exogenous variables, such as Europe and the global economy). What set Macron apart from his immediate predecessors during his first year in office lay in the relative harmony of interaction between these three levels of analysis. In terms of individual attributes – whether understood as personal qualities or symbolic and representative attributes – there appeared to be a better fit between Macron and political leadership than in the case of his two immediate predecessors. During the first twelve months, Emmanuel Macron invested the presidency – an established but rather tired political office – with renewed energy and strengthened the claim to understanding leadership, from a strategic institutionalist perspective, as a process of control of one institution over another (Elgie, 1995). During the first year in office, also, the combination of a dynamic leadership and a strengthened office enhanced the position of President Macron in terms of the macro-level: hence the ability to conceive of European, international and global economic pressures as more than simply external constraints, but also as a set of endogenous opportunities. For a while, President Macron ensured that these three essential dimensions of leadership were mutually self-reinforcing. The first year in office offered a relatively rare period of leadership coherence. By the end of this period, however, there were some signs of diminishing leadership returns and unresolved tensions. Part of the problem lay in the heart of the Macron enterprise itself, which is built on rejection of the main party families and difficulty in defining a core political project. This ambivalence now leads us to make a set of concluding judgements.

Conclusion: Emmanuel Macron and the remaking of France

HAS Macron changed the course of French politics? There are methodological dangers in drawing any too-firm conclusions. These are in part inherent in the 'great man' version of history, where a focus on the individual ignores deeper forces and underlying heavy variables. They are also temporally contingent; the observed period is a short one, undoubtedly too short to permit firm conclusions. Taking these limitations into account, this conclusion now presents an interpretation of President Macron's leadership and engages in some conjecture about the future.

It is not difficult to formulate a favourable interpretation of Macron's presidency. Its most obvious strengths lay in the symbolic function of Macron himself as a young, dynamic president and the representative of a new generation of political leaders. The coherence of Macron's enterprise should be acknowledged. During the 2017 election campaign, Macron positioned himself very clearly in relation to debates on globalisation, the EU, modernisation and economic reforms, in a manner that justified Wel's analysis that identifies broad continuities with the New Labour project of the late 1990s (economic reform married with social justice, a resolutely pro-European message, investment in education, emphasis on responsibilities and individual merit, challenging interests that mar France's economic success). The extraordinary election of 2017 opened up a dual policy and political window of opportunity: politically, with the trade unions demobilised and the opposition parties de-legitimised, the moment was ripe to push reforms through; and in terms of policy very few sectors were left untouched by the ambitious programme of the first year. The result was one of the most ambitious reform programmes of the Fifth Republic – on the face of it, at least. The record after the first year in office was impressive. LR politicians in particular were in a dilemma because many LR electors approved the main measures undertaken by Macron, such as the reform of the labour market.

That Macron represents a form of renewal is one of the least controversial interpretations of his leadership (Sirinelli, 2017). Baudry, Bigorne and Duhamel (2017) interpret renewal in terms of changing the existing political caste, rejecting traditional party politics and contesting the pertinence of the left–right cleavage. In his analysis of the new parliament elected in June 2017, Ollion (2017) identified a generational renewal, evidenced by the age of the LRM deputies, their political inexperience and the passing of political age of the baby boom generation. Macron's election can also be interpreted as a broader sociological renewal, as more women, business people and professionals have entered into government and parliament. In her analysis of Macron's lexicography, Darrigand (2017) adds an additional dimension and interprets renewal in terms similar to Mélenchon's *dégagisme*, referring to the wholescale replacement of existing political elites.

The very fact of Macron's election contradicted the view of the journalist Jean-Michel Apathie (2016) that 'we take almost the same people and start all over again'. In fairness, this editorial reflected the consensus view amongst many editorialists of the time that the 2017 contest would probably be a replay of that of 2012, with Hollande against Sarkozy. Macron was a surprise, a novelty, a fresh prospect, though he had been a key player at the heart of Hollande's administration since 2012 (as either advisor or minister). Rather like Sarkozy in 2007, Macron was able to frame his political appeal as being against the tired old system and its elites, though having been part of the old world that he condemned. Rather like Sarkozy, also, the president with his sheer energy encapsulated public opinion and commentators alike for the first year of his presidential term. Far more than Sarkozy, Macron was given the benefit of the doubt by a public opinion – resigned or curious, rather than enthusiastic – which accepted that the time for reform had come, or at least that the new president had clearly announced what he intended to do. Most French electors supported Macron's attempt to reform the SNCF, in spite of several months of railway strikes. For the first year, at least, Macron was given the benefit of the doubt. He was able to withstand unpopularity, as he was sure not to face any nation-wide elections before the European election of June 2019. For an ostensibly apolitical president, moreover, Macron displayed great strategic astuteness in weakening political rivals.

During the period under observation, Macron benefited from a favourable set of circumstances, with an overall presidential majority, the absence of an effective opposition and a vacuum of leadership in France's main partners. Thus far, there had been little practical opposition to Macron: the veteran left-wing leader Mélenchon was forced to admit that Macron had 'won the first round' as attempts to mobilise against the labour market reform fell flat; the PS, a shadow of its former self, was engaged in a process of introspection and leadership selection; the FN, having already suffered a split, engineered a name change (Rassemblement National, or National Rally) in the hope of recapturing its dynamism of the 2012–17 period; the Republicans barely revived at all under their new leader Laurent Wauquiez, as the inheritor party of the UMP was deserted by some of its centrist and centre-right elements and electors; finally, the trade unions were more divided and ineffective than ever. The window of opportunity for reform remained open. But tensions became increasingly apparent, especially as the Macron presidency entered its second year.

Macron's leadership style: an interpretation

We understand 'leadership style' to refer to the complex mix of preferences, beliefs, skills, values and practices of individuals in leadership situations (either in terms of these as office-holders or in terms of relations between leaders and followers). There are two principal means of contextualising this style: by reference to analytical models in the leadership literature, and by diachronic comparison with previous French presidents who exercised office under fundamentally similar conditions. To take the first approach, does Macron represent a form of transforming leadership, in the schema of Burns (1978)? He is goal-driven and methodical, and has demonstrated much consistency between his campaign pledges and his practice. Transforming leadership is defined by Burns (1978) as a form of uplifting moral leadership which is not merely goal-driven, but also inspirational and charismatic. The transformational leader is not a 'mere' power-wielder, but exercises a force of moral, values-based leadership, which cements exceptionally close leader–follower relations. In practice, the bar is placed high, too high indeed for most empirical cases of leadership in regulated institutional environments. The metaphor of transformational leadership exaggerates the coherence and originality of the Macron enterprise, as well as the likely depth of the policy transformations put into place.

A weaker definition of transformation might allow us to adopt a more nuanced interpretation. In her analysis of 'the ten words that best characterise Macron', Darrigand prefers 'transformation' to 'revolution' (though *Revolution* was the title of Macron's successful 2016 book). 'Transformation' refers to an ambitious programme of gradual reforms, the cumulative effect of which would to transform society. Transformation is most definitely preferred in the Macron lexicography either to revolution (a utopian vision removed from reality and producing dystopian outcomes) or to reform (a negative truism, associated with disillusion on account of the failure of successive governments to reform French society). It is progressive and pragmatic. Transformation is viewed by Macron as a form of correction of past errors, of unblocking the numerous blockages of French politics, society and economy and liberating energies, while protecting the weakest in society (Macron, 2016b).

The real test lies in the ability to evaluate whether Macron's reforms have produced transformational change. While this is clearly premature, the rhythm of the announced reforms in general has been more convincing that their substantive content (which ought to be interpreted in terms of a series of institutional modifications, modest changes in the fiscal system and an unwillingness to cut deep into public expenditure in spite of favourable economic circumstances in 2017–18). If Macron benefited initially from the global upturn in the world economy and the efforts of his predecessor Hollande to restore the public finances, there remain questions about how to fund some of his campaign promises, such as the abolition of local taxes for most of the population, the introduction of a massive investment programme, the reintroduction of a form of national service and making unemployment benefit available to independents and small business owners.

The transformation analogy makes most sense insofar as it is opposed to the figure of the transactional leader in Burns's classical model. In the Macron administration, there is a weak culture of negotiation and a determination to avoid the logic of transaction. All parties might have been involved in round-table talks over the labour reform, for example, but such partnership was limited to negotiating details of implementation, rather than genuinely co-producing public policy. The reform of the national railway, the SNCF, and the legal statute of railway workers was announced as a big bang, for example, rather than a compromise as a result of negotiation.

Rather than refer to abstract models, it makes more sense to situate Macron in terms of leadership traditions and practices within the French Fifth Republic. The contention is that Macron's presidential style has a syncretic quality, drawing on practices and symbols of past French and foreign presidents. There is a conscious and continuing reference to the practices, routines and gestures of his predecessors, with the seven preceding presidents of the Fifth Republic providing a rich empirical pool for developing a repertoire of presidential action. De Gaulle is the most obvious model, as the general's return to power in May 1958 was followed by a six-month period of governing by decrees (*ordonnances*) and calling on high civil servants (rather than politicians) to govern the country. Self-consciously comparing their actions to those of de Gaulle is a constant of French presidential discourse. There are many similarities between Macron and the early Gaullien period, not least in the negation of party politics and the creation of a presidential movement to support the action of the provident individual; in sum, the de Gaulle heritage for Macron signifies in part a leader against parties and the old cleavages. Macron has also delved deep into the Gaullist register of transcending national divisions and resisting civil society or, more pejoratively, the *corps intermédiaires.*

Next, in terms of significance, drawing from President Giscard d'Estaing (1974–81), Macron demonstrates a youthful modernity and calls to reform a blocked France that aspires to be governed in the national interest beyond left and right. Drawing from President Mitterrand, he proclaims a grand European design, as eloquently presented in the speech to the Sorbonne, following in the steps of Mitterrand over three decades earlier. More recently, there are certain obvious parallels with Sarkozy (2007–12), the hyper-president with a far reach into politics, administration and society. The counter-models are the two 'radical Republican' presidents Chirac (who held a hazardous referendum on the future of the EU) and Hollande, the deliberate anti-model. Beyond France, the most influential models and sources of inspiration are the US presidents Barack Obama and, at a distance once-removed, John Fitzgerald Kennedy.

There is nothing entirely new under the sun, but Macron's leadership goes beyond a careful cultivation of – and respect for – selected predecessors and comparators. Macron's mix might be interpreted in terms of a syncretic leadership style: he draws on ideas from wherever they come and maintains apparent contradictions in a state of tension. Hence he moves from Hegelian philosopher to Radical pragmatist without fear of contradiction. We sound a note of caution: the capacity to mobilise a broad range of literary and philosophical references may say more about Macron's educational trajectory – *hypokhâghne,*[1] Sciences Po, ENA – and the capacity for synthesis produced by the educational elite than it does about the erudite personality itself.

How does Macron compare with Hollande? Gaffney (2015) identifies five types of leadership traits within the leadership setting of the Fifth Republic: characterical capital traits (the claim for leadership as a quality setting the individual apart from others); generic leadership traits (qualities more or less required by the office); cultural character traits (linked to the myths of leadership in a particular situation); real traits (those that are displayed by particular individuals); and new traits (particular practices introduced at one moment or another into the overarching presidential leadership style). These five traits might be simplified into those specifically related to an individual politician (style) and those related to the presidential office, its symbols and its practices (role), though in practice there is considerable interaction between the two categories. Style is not purely individual, but is built on a repertoire of received presidential gestures and responses that are mobilised to suit particular situations. Role is not a purely a static reception of the office, and can accommodate the mobilisation of traits in a somewhat eclectic fashion, as illustrated well by Sarkozy, who shifted from the vulgar to the presidential register, or Hollande, who was able to rise above being normal with his reaction to the terrorist attacks of 2015, which saw him adopt the role of father of the nation in a convincing manner.

The received view of Hollande's style was one of slow, ponderous, indecisive leadership, reflecting his past as a party leader more attuned to engineering compromises in party conferences than to engaging in the exercise of power. Various biographies – those of Amar (2014) and Davet and Lhomme (2016) in particular – have disseminated this view, and it was most brutally expressed by Hollande's former partner Valérie Trierweiler (2014), who also portrayed him as a socially callous individual (mocking the poor as the 'toothless' – 'les sans-dents' – largely responsible for their own fate). This view was not, of course, that disseminated by Hollande himself in his best-selling *Les leçons du pouvoir*. Even Hollande, however, recognised retrospectively the shortcomings of his construction of the normal president, which was misunderstood by an important fraction of the population and fell short of the construction of the presidency as an 'elective monarchy' (Hollande, 2018: 26–28). A common image of Hollande was that

of the accidental president, fortuitously seizing unforeseen circumstances, though this view underestimated his determination
in the view of one former minister interviewed in 2013. History
may look more kindly on Hollande, who made a dignified exit
from the scene in December 2016, but for many for the former
president symbolised not only the deliquescence of French Socialism, but also the poor fit between individual political style and
the demands of the presidential office. On balance, Hollande
performed less well than his successor against the benchmark
of generic leadership traits, while Macron initially excelled in
terms of situating his leadership in the context of Fifth Republic
leadership traditions.

Macron deliberately constructed his political style to be the
counter-model to that of Hollande. Well before his election as
president, he identified a broad-based nostalgia for the monarchy,
or at least a desire for strong, rather mystical leadership that
would build on the Gaullist–Mitterrandien framing of the presidency as well as the legacy of the monarchy, or the two Bonapartist
empires. Consequently, he advocated a vertical form of governing:
the President of the Republic ought to be remote, above the fray
and exceptional, rather than normal. During the early months of
his presidency, Macron encouraged the diffusion of the image
of Jupiter, the god of gods in Roman mythology, providing direction
and authoritative leadership (Ignazi, 2018). At the same time, in
this vision the leader is seen as akin to the head of a commando
determined to shake up and reform French and European politics
(Lévrier, 2018). In this leadership-focused venture, personal loyalty
is valued as a core quality, and personal relationships have a
transcendental quality. A tightly knit band of followers (Ismaël
Emelien, Julien de Normandie, Christophe Castaner and Alexis
Kohler, *inter alia*) played the role of first-generation Israeli sabras,
absolutely devoted to their leader and acting as guarantors of
the core legitimacy of Macronism and gatekeepers to Macron
himself. All in all, Macron displayed a rather more conventional
form of presidential leadership than either Sarkozy or Hollande
and came closer to the embodiment of the presidential office

than his three immediate predecessors. Insofar as Macron's leadership is partly syncretic, it is more in line with the spirit of the Fifth Republic than that of Hollande —especially – and possibly than that of Sarkozy as well.

Understanding the Macron project

The Macron project is above all a hybrid political and economic project. Macron has set out to reaffirm the centrality of the presidency and rehabilitate the discourse of the State. His presidential practice has renewed with traditional visions of the Fifth Republic, whereby the president is at the heart of a centripetal and hierarchical system. President Macron has been involved in almost everything: for example, appointments in the public-sector media, the functioning of the justice system, the details of economic management, movements in the civil service and so on. Combining the various roles he has assumed (from Jupiterian president internally to global brand abroad) is literally exhausting, with presidential advisors reputedly in a state of burn-out. The important role performed by Macron in global politics has left little time for domestic coordination. There is no substantive presidential party on which to rely to diffuse the presidential message and disseminate support. Above all, Macron's decision-making system has relied on personal loyalty and on individual centrality, with the risk of a loss of balance when times are less favourable. During the first year, he was present on all fronts, but the over-exposure showed signs of becoming a source of weakness. The success of Macron's presidency will depend in part on whether this vision is performative, whether it guides the actions of others and produces transformation.

If the tide turns, the Jupiter metaphor may also give rise to ridicule. There is a danger of falling into the trap of Hubris, described by Owen and Davidson (2009: 1346) as a sense of 'exaggerated pride, overwhelming self-confidence and a contempt for others'. The positive qualities of leadership – such as charisma, charm, persuasiveness, decisiveness and self-confidence – can in their turn produce more negative qualities of impetuosity, a refusal to listen to or to take advice, impulsiveness, recklessness and inattention to detail. These dangers are especially associated with the Bonapartist style, a form of grandiose decision-making that ignores the role of intermediaries and postulates a direct quasi-monarchical relationship between leader and led. In the UK and US contexts, 'hubris' has been used to describe rulers such as Thatcher, Blair and Bush. Might it also apply to this brash newcomer? The Benalla scandal of July 2018 was potentially so damaging because it suggested that Macron was not living up to his principles; his refusal of castes or special privileges appeared not to apply in the case of his own presidential advisors.

Borrowing an analogy from economics, some interpretations of political leadership have emphasised diminishing leadership returns, as early political capital is gradually exhausted, political resources are consumed, and reform efforts wither (Gaffney, 2015; Cole, 1994). As the second year began in earnest, more problematic reforms lay on the agenda: of pensions and the civil service, constitutional reform and making good promises made to Brussels in terms of reducing public debt and bringing down public spending. On the anniversary of Macron's election, public opinion was wavering. Macron's disruptive or transgressive style was increasingly perceived as provocative (as in the remark about the 'mad amount of money' ('pognon de dingue') made in an online video in relation to social expenditure, 'Macron s'enflamme', 2018) and sometimes even callous. The *en même temps* slogan appeared less and less convincing in terms of domestic politics, where the actions of the Philippe government were interpreted by public opinion as being 'of the right'. In terms of EU and foreign politics, Macron's EU agenda was disrupted by the migrant crisis and relations with other governments such as that of Italy. The economic outlook was markedly less optimistic, as a trans-Atlantic trade war loomed. These various dimensions underline the contingent nature of leadership and the difficulties of formulating an overall appreciation, which must nonetheless be attempted.

One influential representation of Macron is that of the philosopher Chantal Mouffe, for whom Macron appears as a post-political entrepreneur (Mouffe, 2017). For this philosopher close to Mélenchon, Macron was the genuine inheritor of Blair's Third Way, interpreted as a confiscation of democratic alternatives behind the doctrine of universal values and the lack of an alternative to orthodox neo-liberal economic policy. In a rather similar vein, Matyjasik (2018) writes of politics without values, of a leader with a cult of managerial performance. These perspectives tell us at least as much about their promoters (and their ideological leanings) as they do about Macron himself. The description of Macron as a post-political entrepreneur captures one important dimension of his leadership, however. As candidate and then president, Macron declared himself to be openly distrustful of parties and politics, and he surfed the wave of anti-party politics to great effect in 2017. He came to power against the parties. Far from traditional political jousts, since Macron's election a rather technocratic language of modernisation has prevailed as the leitmotif of governmental action.

Macron's presidency has already acted as an accelerator of deep trends afoot in the governing and governance of France, though the pattern is still blurred and somewhat uneven. Initially formulated by Jobert and Muller (1987) in their classic study of French public policy, the model of republican corporatism describes the French policy style in terms of a compromise between a strong state direction (the republican dimension, especially in the economy) and the management of public services by the professions (the corporatist dimension, best captured by the role of the employers, the trade unions and the regulated professions in managing the post-war social security system). In a previous work (Cole, 2008), I identified a French-style governance, whereby this traditional model had already been modified by the impact of decentralisation, the weakening of the state in the economy, Europeanisation, the private delivery of public goods and the invention of new instruments of governmental steering. Three dimensions of France's model of republican corporatism have been further challenged under Macron.

First, by reforms in the field of labour markets, training and unemployment insurance and in general patterns of collective bargaining, Macron has clearly signalled his intention to limit the role of social partners (employers and trade unions) as co-managers of the French welfare state. The economic justification is the liberal one of making markets more fluid and rewarding enterprise, while Macron's political liberalism is built on emphasising transparency and accountability. There are powerful resource-based arguments to pursue this path, not least in removing the direct control of the social partners in the management of the French training and unemployment insurance systems (including an attack on the funding mechanisms (*organismes paritaires de collecte agrées*, OPCA) that are important sources of revenue for the employers and trade unions). Macron has renewed with the early Gaullien discourse critical of the *corps intermédiaires*, framed in terms of obstacles to the ability of a progressive-minded government to reform France and reverse its decline.

Second, as illustrated in Chapter 5, Macron has looked to central government in general – and the technocratic elite in particular – as the key to unblocking the blocked society (Cos, 2017). One by-product has been the weakening of the territorial dimension of French-style governance. The professional local government associations have complained of being excluded from the previously comfortable arrangements with the government in terms of co-constructing policies affecting local government. Reforms of the training and apprenticeship systems have overlooked the regional councils, though they have developed competencies over many years. Above all, local and regional authorities have been put under pressure to agree to a new system of contractualisation over the 2018–22 period, whereby they commit to control expenditure and remain within overall ceilings on public expenditure (as part of the announced reduction of thirteen billion euros over the *quinquennat*). How far will this go? Will it involve rolling back key elements of the decentralisation reforms of 1982?

Third, there is tension between the vertical practices associated with Macron as president and the horizontal frame of a stable, deliberative democracy that was theorised during the campaign. Doubts have been expressed in relation to Macron's view of the democratic process in general, by erstwhile friends such as Jean-Paul Huchon, former president of the Île-de-France region (who was close to the former premier Michel Rocard and critical of Macron's sidelining of voluntary associations and social partners), as well as confirmed opponents, such as the president of the Senate, Gérard Larcher. The proposed constitutional reform, announced in detail on 9 April 2018, was based on streamlined version of democracy: fewer parliamentarians, few career politicians, more focus on processes of scrutiny and the implementation of centrally designed objectives.

Macron's leadership represents above all a strengthening of central steering and of the personalised governance that is facilitated by the presidential institutions of the Fifth Republic. The paradox, in the expression of Perrineau (2018), is that 'the man who presented himself as an adept of a horizontal management style, as in the start-up culture, in fact governs in a vertical, top-down manner'. Perhaps observers ought not to be too surprised. Let us not forget that before becoming president, Macron was a highly interventionist economy minister, notably in terms of frustrating the announced merger of the mobile telephone operator SFR and the property and telecommunications conglomerate Bouygues, or again in interfering in operations of the car maker Renault (indeed, creating diplomatic pressures with Japan by raising the French State's stake in the company) (Cole, 2017). The second year brought the dangers and potentially counter-productive aspects of Macron's approach to the fore. Macron's reference to Jupiter conveyed the image of a president above the fray, above the routine competition of parties and alone vested with supreme decision-making authority, but the 2018 edition of the CEVIPOF's annual survey (*Fractures françaises*) revealed mistrust of the presidency to be on the rise again (Courtois et al., 2018). The Macron effect was starting to wither even before the Benalla scandal brought into the public domain the dysfunctional dimensions of Macron's leadership: secrecy, lack of transparency, double standards and excessive personalisation.

Looking forward

The two years that changed France were years of unease and instability in international relations (the war against so-called Islamic State, the turmoil in the Middle East), in trans-Atlantic relations (the election of Trump as US president in November 2016), in the EU (the Brexit referendum of June 2016). Various alternative scenarios of France's future circulated during the 2017 elections, from the apocalyptic (Le Pen) to the romantic (Mélenchon, Hamon) and the austere (Fillon), before settling on Macron's carefully constructed equilibrium. One year into Macron's presidency, even the thickest-skinned 'declinologists', such as Nicolas Baverez, writing in Le Point (2017), were more resolutely upbeat about French politics, society and economy than they had ever been.

There remains a lingering question over whether the 'old world' is really dead. There has, certainly, been an overhaul in political personnel, and almost all the main parties have undergone name changes. Added to the state of public opinion, the organisational structures underpinning the traditional left–right battle have been fractured; the PS, under new leader Olivier Faure, is reduced to its core strongholds in local and regional government; LFI has, thus far, been unable to mobilise opposition to the Macron regime; LR is sorely divided, with the remnants of the centre-right pro-European wing of the movement considering its future in an increasingly eurosceptical movement under Wauquiez; the FN or Rassemblement National might revive, but Marine Le Pen's leadership is contested. Various scenarios are possible, consideration of which lie beyond this book. The danger with the hollowing-out of traditional left–right politics concerns what might be put in its place. What would happen if the central space itself became hollowed out in a reaction to modernising French society and the failure to reshape European integration? What would replace Macron, given the withering-away of traditional parties and the inability of new ones to structure the political space? Is the populist menace really over? The feared second-round showdown between Marine Le Pen and Jean-Luc Mélenchon did not materialise ... but it might have done. And the blurring of the traditional frontiers between left and right – which in part explained Macron's success in France – has taken more radical forms in countries such as, *inter alia*, Italy (where the Five Star Movement and the League have joined forces to lead the government) and Austria (where the far-right has been bought into coalition) and might conceivably produce continuing volcanic tremors in France itself. Though existing party structures have been weakened, the new movements – such as LRM, LFI and others – have not yet been fully tested or demonstrated themselves to be capable of structuring the political space. Clearly, the danger is that of a void, or a 'populist' reaction to a hollowed-out centre. The real test of Macron's political leadership will come at the end of his first presidential term. Definitive-sounding comments today, made from the vantage point of the first twelve months in power, may look foolish by the end of the Macron presidency. All that we can say with confidence is that the making of Emmanuel Macron is a prelude to his unmaking at some point in the future.

Note

1   Referring to a system of preparatory schools for entry into prestigious institutions such as the École Normale Supérieure or Sciences Po, the *hypokhâghne* provide an education centred on literature, the classics and philosophy.

References

Abel, O. (2017) 'Le politique et le philosophe: Emmanuel Macron et Paul Ricœur', *Études*, 4241 (September): 47–57.

Ahlquist, J. S., and Levi, M. (2011) 'Leadership: What it Means, What it Does, and What we Want to Know About it', *Annual Review of Political Science*, 14: 1–24.

Amar, Cécile (2014) *Jusqu'à ici ou va mal*, Paris: Grasset.

Apathie, Jean-Michel (2016) *On prend (presque) les mêmes et on recommence*, Paris: Flammarion.

Barboni, T. (2009) 'Le Parti socialiste, parti de militants, des militants ... ou de supporters?', *Recherche socialiste*, 46–7: 13–25.

Baudry, Alice, Bigorne, Laurent, and Duhamel, Olivier (2017) *Macron, et en même temps*, Paris: Plon.

Baverez, Nicolas (2013) *Réveillez-vous*, Paris: Pluriel.

Baverez, Nicolas (2017) 'La France, promesse de l'aube', *Le Point*, 25 December.

Beaud, O. (2016) 'Ce projet de réforme constitutionnelle est inutile et inepte', *Le Monde*, 2 February.

Bekmezian, H. (2016) 'Le Sénat enterre la déchéance de la nationalité', *Le Monde*, 19 March.

Bell, David, S., and Gaffney, John (eds) (2013) *Political Leadership in France: From Charles de Gaulle to Nicolas Sarkozy*, Basingstoke: Palgrave.

Belouezzane, S. (2017) 'Le subtil jeu d'équilibre des cabinets ministériels', *Le Monde*, 28 May.

Berrington, H. (1974) 'The fiery chariot: British Prime Ministers and the search for love', *British Journal of Political Science*, 4 (3): 345–369.

Besson, Philippe (2017) *Un personnage de roman*, Paris: Juillard.

BFM TV (2018) 'Qui a tué Francois Fillon?', 29 January.

Blondel, Jean (1987) *Political Leadership*, London: Sage.

Bonnefous, B., Pietralunga, C., and de Royer, S. (2017) 'Macron, une gouvernance en mode secret', *Le Monde*, 11 May.

Botella, J. (2018) 'Sondage exclusif You Gov: 71% des Français opposés aux 80 km/h sur route nationale', *Capital*, 25 May, https:// www.capital.fr/economie-politique/sondage-exclusif-yougov- 71-des-francais-opposes-aux-80-km-h-sur-route-nationale-1289782 (last accessed 10 October 2018).

Bourmaud, François-Xavier (2017a) *Emmanuel Macron – les coulisses d'une victoire*, Paris: L'Archipel.

Bourmaud, François-Xavier (2017b) 'La République en marche en plein doute', *Le Figaro*, 15 November.

Buisson, Patrick (2016) *La cause du peuple*, Paris: Perrin.

Burns, James-McGregor (1978) *Leadership*, New York: Harper Collins.

Camby, J.-P. (2018) '1958–2018: évolutions ou révolutions du travail parlementaire', *Revue politique et parlementaire*, 119 (1085–1086): 103–110.

Camus, J.-Y. (2011) 'Le processus de normalisation des droites radicales en Europe', *Cités*, 45 (1): 153–156.

Capdevielle, Jacques (ed.) (1981) *France de gauche, vote à droite*, Paris: Presses de la FNSP.

Chabal, Émile (2015) *A Divided Republic: Nation, State and Citizenship in Contemporary France*, Cambridge: Cambridge University Press.

Charlot, J. (1983) 'Le président et le parti majoritaire: du Gaullisme au socialisme', *Revue politique et parlementaire*, 85 (905): 27–40.

Cheurfa, M. (2017) 'Les exceptions à la confiance politique', in *Baromètre de la confiance politique 8* (Paris: CEVIPOF), www.cevipof.com/ fr/le-barometre-de-la-confiance-politique-du-cevipof/resultats-1/ vague8/ (last accessed 24 July 2017).

Cole, Alistair (1989) 'Factionalism, the French Socialist Party and the Fifth Republic: An Explanation of Intra-Party Divisions', *European Journal of Political Research*, 17 (1): 77–94.

Cole, Alistair (1994) *François Mitterrand: A Study in Political Leadership*, London: Routledge.

Cole, Alistair (2008) *Governing and Governance in France*, Cambridge: Cambridge University Press.

Cole, Alistair (2012) 'The Fast Presidency? Nicolas Sarkozy and the Political Institutions of the Fifth Republic', *Contemporary French and Francophone Studies*, 16 (3): 311–321.

Cole, Alistair (2014) 'Not Saying, Not Doing: Convergences, Contingencies and Causal Mechanisms of State Reform and Decentralisation in Hollande's France', *French Politics*, 12 (2): 104–135.

Cole, Alistair (2016) 'Bye Bye Mr Sarkozy, Hello Mr Nobody', *Presidential Power*, 29 November, http://presidential-power.com/?p=5677 (last accessed 5 August 2018).

Cole, Alistair (2017) *French Politics and Society*, London: Routledge.

Cole, Alistair, Meunier, Sophie, and Tiberj, Vincent (eds) (2013) *Developments in French Politics 5*, Basingstoke: Palgrave.

Collectif Léa Guessier (2018) 'La haute administration, véritable parti présidentiel', *Le Monde*, 22 February.

Cos, R. (2017) 'Idéologiquement, Macron a fait du neuf avec du vieux', *Le Monde*, 25–26 May.

Courtois, G. (2018) 'L'optimisme post-élection de Macron s'est dissipé', *Le Monde*, 10 July.

Courtois, G., Finchelstein, G., Foucault, M., and Teinturier, B. (2018) *Fractures françaises 2018*, Paris: Fondation Jean Jaurès.

Couturier, Bruno (2017) *Macron: un président philosophe*, Paris: Éditions de l'Observatoire.

Crépon, Sylvain, Dézé, Alexandre, and Mayer Nonna (eds) (2015) *Les faux semblants du Front national: sociologie d'un parti politique*, Paris: Presses de Sciences Po.

Crouch, Colin (2013) *Post-Democracy*, Cambridge: Polity Press.

Darrigand, M. (2017) 'Emmanuel Macron en dix mots', *Études*, 4241 (September): 21–32.

Davet, Gérard, and Lhomme, Fabrice (2016) *Un président ne devrait pas dire ça ...*, Paris: Stock.

de Maillard, Jacques, and Surel, Yves (eds) (2012) *Les politiques publiques sous Sarkozy*, Paris: Presses de Sciences Po.

de Montvalon, J.-B. (2016) 'Nicolas Sarkozy porté par la dynamique de sa campagne', *Le Monde*, 27 September.

de Royer, S. (2017) 'Emmanuel Macron: la technocratie au pouvoir', *Le Monde*, 7 November.

de Royer, S. (2018) 'Le président people et le miroir aux alouettes', *Le Monde*, 16 March.

de Waele, Jean-Michel, and Seiler, Daniel-Louis (eds) (2012) *Les partis de la gauche anticapitaliste en Europe*, Paris: Economica.

Debray, Régis (2017) *Le nouveau pouvoir*, Paris: Éditions du Cerf.

Derrien, Candice, and Nedelec, Caroline (2017) *Les Macron*, Paris: Fayard.

Dive, Bruno (2016) *Alain Juppé: l'homme qui revient de loin*, Paris: L'Archipel.

Drake, Helen (2000) *Jacques Delors: Perspectives on a European Leader*, London: Routledge.

Drake, Helen (2011) *Contemporary France*, Basingstoke: Palgrave.

Drake, Helen (2013) 'France and the European Union', in Alistair Cole, Sophie Meunier and Vincent Tiberj (eds), *Developments in French Politics 5*, Basingstoke: Palgrave, pp. 218–232.

Dyson, K. (1999) 'Benign or Malevolent Leviathan? Social-Democratic Governments in a Neo-Liberal "Euro-Area"', *Political Quarterly*, 70 (2): 195–209.

Edinger, L. J. (1990) 'Approaches to the Comparative Analysis of Political Leadership', *Review of Politics*, 52 (4): 509–523.

ELABE (2017) 'Intentions de vote – élection présidentielle 2017', https://elabe.fr/intentions-de-vote-election-presidentielle-2017-15/ (last accessed 12 October 2018).

ELABE (2018) 'Mobilisations sociales: un souhait d'inflexion de la politique actuelle?', https://elabe.fr/mobilisations-sociales-inflexion-politique/ (last accessed 9 October 2018).

ELABE–BFM (2017) 'Primaires citoyennes: comprendre le vote (premier tour)', 22 January, https://elabe.fr/comprendre-le-vote-3/ (last accessed 8 October 2018).

Elgie, Robert (1995) *Political Leadership in Liberal Democracies*, Basingstoke, Palgrave Macmillan.

Elgie, Robert (2000) *Semi-Presidentialism in Europe*, Oxford: Oxford University Press.

Elgie, Robert, Grossman, Emiliano, and Mazur, Amy (eds) (2016) *The Oxford Handbook of French Politics*, Oxford: Oxford University Press.

Escalona, F. (2017) 'The Terminal Collapse of the French Socialist Party', www.academia.edu/33467816/The_terminal_collapse_of_the_French_Socialist_Party (last accessed 13 October 2018).

Escalona, F., and Vieira, M. (2014) 'Le sens et le rôle de l'opposition à l'UE du Parti de Gauche', *Politique européenne*, 43: 31–54.

Evans, J. (2018) 'La candidature de Macron et le mouvement En marche!', in Riccardo Brizzi and Marc Lazar (eds), *La France d'Emmanuel Macron*, Rennes: Presses Universitaires de Rennes, pp. 83–102.

Faye, O., and Goar, M. (2017) 'Sens commun, l'encombrant ami des Républicains', *Le Monde*, 14 October.

Le Figaro (2016) 'Pour Nicolas Sarkozy, "dès que l'on devient Français, nos ancêtres sont Gaulois"', Agence France Presse, 20 September.

Fillon, François (2016) *Vaincre le terrorisme Islamiste*, Paris: Albin Michel.

Foley, M. (2009) 'Gordon Brown and the Role of Compounded Crisis in the Pathology of Leadership Decline', *British Politics*, 4 (4): 498–513.

Frachon, A. (2017) 'Global Macron', *Le Monde*, 12 May.

Fressoz, F. (2017) 'La puissance plutôt que la toute-puissance', *Le Monde*, 18 July.

Fulda, Anne (2016) *Emmanuel Macron, un jeune homme si parfait*, Paris: Plon.

Gaffney, John (2013) 'Charles de Gaulle: The Real Gaullist Settlement', in David S. Bell and John Gaffney (eds), *Political Leadership in*

France: From Charles de Gaulle to Nicolas Sarkozy, Basingstoke: Palgrave, pp. 79–97.

Gaffney, John (2015) *France in the Hollande Presidency: The Unhappy Republic*, Basingstoke: Palgrave.

Gaxie, D. (2012) 'Tous les électeurs ne s'intéressent pas aux mêmes problèmes', interview, *Mediapart.fr*, 15 May, http://blogs.mediapart.fr/edition/sociologie-politique-des-elections/article/060212/tous-les-electeurs-ne-sinteressent-pas-aux-mêmes-problèmes (last accessed 13 August 2017).

Geai, L. (2017) 'Qu'est-ce que l'alliance bolivarienne pour les Amériques évoquée par Mélenchon?', *Le Monde*, 14 April.

Gervasoni, M. (2018) 'Une "défaite normale": le crépescule des socialistes?', in Riccardo Brizzi and Marc Lazar (eds), *La France d'Emmanuel Macron*, Rennes: Presses Universitaires de Rennes, pp. 149–172.

Goar, Matthieu (2016) 'La semaine où Sarkozy a été rattrapé par son passé', *Le Monde*, 30 September.

Goar, Matthieu (2017) *Francois Fillon: les coulisses d'une défaite*, Paris: L'Archipel.

Grunberg, G. (2011) 'Le parti d'Épinay: d'une rupture fantasmée à un réformisme mal assumé', *Histoire@politique*, 13: 1–12.

Grunberg, G., and Haegel, F. (2018) 'Le temps des primaires', in Riccardo Brizzi and Marc Lazar (eds), *La France d'Emmanuel Macron*, Rennes: Presses Universitaires de Rennes, pp. 41–56.

Guilluy, Christophe (2014) *La France périphérique: comment on a sacrifié les classes populaires*, Paris: Flammarion.

Guisnel, J. (2018) 'Comment Macron fait la guerre', *Le Point*, 5 July.

Haegel, F. (2013) 'Political Parties: The UMP and the Right', in Alistair Cole, Sophie Meunier and Vincent Tiberj (eds), *Developments in French Politics 5*, Basingstoke: Palgrave, pp. 88–103.

Hanley, D. (2013) 'Political Leadership: from the Fourth to the Fifth Republic', in David S. Bell and John Gaffney, *Political Leadership in France: From Charles de Gaulle to Nicolas Sarkozy*, Basingstoke: Palgrave, pp. 27–43.

Hayward, J. (2013) '"Hyperpresidentialism" and the Fifth Republic State Imperative', in David S. Bell and John Gaffney (eds), *Political*

Leadership in France: From Charles de Gaulle to Nicolas Sarkozy, Basingstoke: Palgrave, pp. 44–57.

Helms, L. (1996) 'Executive Leadership in Parliamentary Democracies: The British Prime Minister and the German Chancellor Compared', *German Politics*, 5 (1): 101–120.

Hollande, François (2018) *Les leçons du pouvoir*, Paris: Stock.

Howorth, J. (2013) 'French Foreign and Security Policy: In Search of Coherence and Impact', in Alistair Cole, Sophie Meunier and Vincent Tiberj (eds), *Developments in French Politics 5*, Basingstoke: Palgrave, pp. 250–266.

Hughes, P. (2018) 'Le pari européen de Merkel', *Le Point*, 8 March.

Ignazi, P. (2018) 'Emmanuel Macron entre Jupiter et Minerve', in Riccardo Brizzi and Marc Lazar (eds), *La France d'Emmanuel Macron*, Rennes: Presses Universitaires de Rennes, pp. 195–216.

IPSOS–CEVIPOF–*Le Monde* (2016) 'François Hollande dans une position toujours plus difficile avant la Présidentielle', 30 March, www.ipsos.fr/decrypter-societe/2016-03-30-francois-hollande-dans-position-toujours-plus-difficile-avant-presidentielle (last accessed 7 August 2018).

Irondelle, B., Joana, J., and Mérand, F. (2016) 'Defense and Security Policy: Beyond French Exceptionalism', in Robert Elgie, Emiliano Grossman and Amy Mazur (2016) (eds), *The Oxford Handbook of French Politics* Oxford: Oxford University Press, pp. 636–653.

Jaffré, J. (2012) 'Ce que signifie le vote du 6 mai', *Le Monde*, 5 June.

Jeanneney, Jean-Noël (2017) *Le moment Macron – un président et l'histoire*, Paris: Seuil.

Jobert, Bruno, and Muller, Pierre (1987) *L'état en action: politiques publiques et corporatisme*, Paris: Presses Universitaires de France.

Journal de Dimanche (2017) 'La personnalité du candidat Macron divise les français', 3092, 19 March.

Juillard, J. (2018) 'Fragilités du Macronisme', *Le Figaro*, 1 July.

Juppé, Alain (2016) *Pour un état fort*, Paris: J. C. Lattes.

Knapp, A. (2018) 'Structure versus Accident in the Defeat of France's Mainstream Right, April–June 2017', *Parliamentary Affairs*, 71 (3): 558–577.

Lazar M. (2018a) 'De quoi le Macronisme est-il le nom?', in Riccardo Brizzi and Marc Lazar (eds), *La France d'Emmanuel Macron*, Rennes: Presses Universitaires de Rennes, pp. 299–308.

Lazar, M. (2018b) 'La surprise Jean-Luc Mélenchon', in Riccardo Brizzi and Marc Lazar (eds), *La France d'Emmanuel Macron*, Rennes: Presses Universitaires de Rennes, pp. 173–194.

Lefebvre, R., and Sawicki, F. (2007) 'Pourquoi le PS ne parle-t-il plus aux catégories populaires?', *Mouvements*, 50 (6–8): 24–41.

Lefebvre, Rémy (2011) *Les primaires socialistes: la fin du parti militant*, Paris: Raisons d'Agir.

Lemarié, A., and Pietralunga, C. (2018) 'La Macronisme, cet objet politique mal identifié', *Le Monde*, 24–25 June.

Lemarié, A., and Rescan, M. (2017) 'Dans les pas des députés En marche!', *Le Monde*, 23–24 July 2017.

Lévrier, A. (2018) 'Les ombres d'une présidence monarchique d'Emmanuel Macron', *Le Monde*, 31 July.

Lewis-Beck, Michael S., Nadeau, Richard, and Bélanger, Eric (2012) *French Presidential Elections*, Basingstoke: Palgrave.

Mack, Charles, S. (2010) *When Political Parties Die: A Cross-National Analysis of Disalignment and Realignment*, Santa Barbara: Praeger.

Macron, Emmanuel (2016a) interview, *Challenges.fr*, https://www.challenges.fr/election-presidentielle-2017/interview-exclusive-d-emmanuel-macron-je-ne-crois-pas-au-president-normal_432886 (last accessed 5 August 2018).

Macron, Emmanuel (2016b) *Révolution*, Paris: XO Éditions.

Macron, Emmanuel (2017) 'Entretien avec Emmanuel Macron', *Le Point*, 31 August.

'Macron s'enflamme' (2018) 'Macron s'enflamme: "On met un pognon de dingue dans les minima sociaux"', https://www.youtube.com/watch?v=rKkUkUFbqmE (last accessed 12 October 2018).

Magnaudeix, M. (2017) 'Dans les rouages de la "Macron Company"', *Mediapart.fr*, 4 February, https://www.mediapart.fr/journal/france/030217/dans-les-rouages-de-la-macron-company?onglet=full (last accessed 13 October 2018).

March, Luke, and Keith, Daniel (eds) (2016) *Europe's Radical Left: From Marginality to the Mainstream?*, London: Rowman and Littlefield.

Marchi, M. (2018) 'La "longue marche" du Front national de Marine Le Pen', in Riccardo Brizzi and Marc Lazar (eds), *La France d'Emmanuel Macron*, Rennes: Presses Universitaires de Rennes, pp. 125–148.

Marshall, P. D., and Barbour, K. (2015) 'Making Intellectual Room for Persona Studies: A New Consciousness and a Shifted Perspective', *Persona Studies*, 1 (1): 1–12.

Martin, Pierre (2000) *Comprendre les évolutions électorales: la théorie des réalignements revisitée*, Paris: Presses de Sciences Po.

Marty, E. (2017) 'L'échec de Le Pen est aussi celui de la stratégie équivoque de Mélenchon', *Le Monde*, 11 May.

Matyjasik, N. (2018) 'La politique d'Emmanuel Macron est une politique sans values', *Libération*, 9 May.

Mongin, O. (2017) 'Les lectures d'Emmanuel Macron', *Commentaire*, 159: 519–523.

Morin, C. (2018) 'Macron, président des très riches. Plus que Sarkozy ou ... Hollande?', *L'Obs*, 5 May.

Moschonas, Gerassimos (2001) *In the Name of Social Democracy: The Great Transformation, 1945 to the Present*, New York: Verso.

Mouffe, C. (2017) 'Le progressisme, en marche ou insoumis', *Le Monde*, 2 June.

Olivier, L. (2009) 'L'identité militante socialiste en question', *Recherche socialiste*, 46–47: 27–41.

Ollion, E. (2017) 'Un sociologue au Palais Bourbon', *Le Monde*, 8 July.

Owen, D., and Davidson, J. (2009) 'Hubris Syndrome: An Acquired Personality Disorder?', *Brain*, 132 (5): 1396–1406.

Parmentier, A. (2017) 'Macron, la troisième voie', *Le Monde*, 3 March.

Pedder, Sophie (2018) *Revolution Française: Emmanuel Macron and the Quest to Reinvent a Nation*, London: Bloomsbury.

Perrineau, P. (2018) 'Emmanuel Macron face à la conversion réformiste du pays', *Le Figaro*, 17 January.

Pierson, Christopher (2001) *Hard Choices: Social Democracy in the 21st Century*, Cambridge: Polity Press.

Pietralunga, C. (2017) 'Entre l'Élysée et Matignon, onze conseillers en commun', *Le Monde*, 18 July.

Pina, C. (2011) 'L'extrême gauche, la vraie gauche?', in Pierre Bréchon (ed.), *Les partis politiques français*, Paris: La Documentation Française, pp. 181–203.

Portelli, Hughes (1980) *Le socialisme français tel qu'il est*, Paris: Presses Universitaires de France.

Prissette, Nicolas (2017) *Emmanuel Macron: le président inattendu*, Paris: First.

Pudal, B. (2004) 'Les communistes', in Jean-Jacques Becker and Gilles Candar (eds), *Histoire des gauches en France*, vol. 2, Paris: Éditions La Découverte, pp. 51–75.

Raffy, Serge (2011) *François Hollande: itinéraire secret*, Paris: Fayard.

Raymond, Gino (ed.) (2013) *The Sarkozy Presidency. Breaking the Mould?*, Basingstoke: Palgrave.

Remond, René (1982) *Les droites en France*, Paris: Aubier.

Reynié. D (2011) 'Le tournant ethno-socialiste du Front national', *Études*, 4155: 463–472.

Richard, Gilles (2017) *Histoire des droites en France (1815–2017)*, Paris: Perrin.

Richard, R. (2017) 'Ce que l'histoire de la droite nous apprend', *Le Point*, 9 March.

Robin, J.-P. (2017) 'Les douze travaux d'Hercule-Macron prendront bien plus qu'un quinquennat', *Le Figaro*, 9 October.

Sauger, N. (2017) 'Raisons et évolution du rejet des partis', *Pouvoirs*, 163: 17–26.

Sawicki, F. (2017) 'L'épreuve du pouvoir est-elle vouée à être fatale au Parti socialiste? *Pouvoirs*, 163: 27–41.

Schweisguth, E. (1983) 'Les couches moyennes salariées sont-elles socialistes?', *Intervention*, 5–6: 58–66.

Shields, J. (2018) 'Electoral Performance and Policy Choices in the Front National', *Parliamentary Affairs*, 71 (3): 538–557.

Sirinelli, Jean-François (2017) *Les révolutions françaises. 1962–2017*, Paris: Odile Jacob.

Smith, M. J. (2007) 'Tony Blair: The First Prime Minister of the Global Era', *British Politics*, 2: 420–427.

Smith, Timothy, B. (2015) *France in Crisis: Welfare, Inequality and Globalisation since 1980*, Cambridge: Cambridge University Press.

Taguieff, Pierre-André (2017) *Macron: miracle ou mirage?*, Paris: Éditions de l'Observatoire.

Tenzer, Nicolas (1998) *La face cachée du gaullisme*, Paris: Hachette.

TF1 (2018) 'Emmanuel Macron – le grand entretien', https://www.tf1.fr/tf1/elections/videos/grand-entretien-e-macron-15-octobre-2017.html (last accessed 10 October 2018).

Touraine, A. (2017) 'Le choix de l'avenir contre celui du passé', *Le Monde*, 2 June.

Trierweiler, V. (2014) *Merci pour ce moment*, Paris: Les Arènes.

Valeurs actuelles (2016) 'Déjà président: Fillon, le triomphe de la droite des valeurs', 24 November.

Weil, P. (2016) 'Le principe d'égalité est un pilier de notre identité', *Le Monde*, 8 January.

Winock, M. (2007) 'Le parti socialiste dans le système politique français', *Vingtième siècle*, 96: 11–12.

Index